# Yesterday on the
# CHESAPEAKE BAY

3/09

*James Tigner, Jr.*

Schiffer Publishing Ltd®

4880 Lower Valley Road  Atglen, Pennsylvania  19310

AUTHORIZED BY ACT OF CONGRESS MAY 19, 1898.

## PRIVATE MAILING CARD
POSTAL CARD (CARTE POSTAL)
THIS SIDE FOR ADDRESS ONLY.

Place
Stamp Here

Domestic
One Cent

Foreign
Two Cents

### ACKNOWLEDGMENTS

THE AUTHOR WISHES TO ACKNOWLEDGE AND THANK THOSE NAMED BELOW, IN ALPHABETICAL ORDER, WHO IN ONE WAY OR ANOTHER LENT THEIR ADVICE, EXPERTISE, WORDS OF ENCOURAGEMENT, OR IN SOME WAY CONTRIBUTED TO THE COMPLETION OF THIS BOOK.

JUDY SHANNON, TINA SKINNER, DAWN TIGNER, ETHEL TIGNER, DAVID A. ZAPPARDINO

**Other Schiffer Books on Related Subjects**

*Greetings From Charleston*, by Mary L. Martin and Nathaniel Wolfgang-Price.

*Memories of Memphis: A History in Postcards,* by Ginny Parfitt and Mary L. Martin

*Baltimore: A History in Postcards,* by Mary L. Martin and Nathaniel Wolfgang-Price

*Wading and Shore Birds of the Atlantic Coast,* by Roger S. Everett

*Upper Chesapeake Bay Decoys and Their Makers*, by David and Joan Hagan.

Copyright © 2007 by James Tigner, Jr.
Library of Congress Control Number:   2006935814

Covers and book designed by: Bruce Waters
Type set in Korinna BT

ISBN: 0-7643-2597-3
Printed in China

Published by Schiffer Publishing Ltd.
4880 Lower Valley Road
Atglen, PA 19310
Phone: (610) 593-1777; Fax: (610) 593-2002
E-mail: Info@schifferbooks.com

For the largest selection of fine reference books on this and related subjects, please visit our web site at **www.schifferbooks.com**
We are always looking for people to write books on new and related subjects.
If you have an idea for a book please contact us at the above address.

This book may be purchased from the publisher.
Include $3.95 for shipping.
Please try your bookstore first.
You may write for a free catalog.

In Europe, Schiffer books are distributed by
Bushwood Books
6 Marksbury Ave.
Kew Gardens
Surrey TW9 4JF England
Phone: 44 (0) 20 8392-8585; Fax: 44 (0) 20 8392-9876
E-mail: info@bushwoodbooks.co.uk
Website: www.bushwoodbooks.co.uk
Free postage in the U.K., Europe; air mail at cost.

# CONTENTS

# INTRODUCTION

This book offers a nostalgic view of what life was like on the Chesapeake Bay during the postcard era. The postcard era was a time frame of approximately six decades, from 1900 to 1960. During that period, the sending and receiving of postcards was a popular thing to do. It was fashionable to trade postcards among friends and also to swap a postcard of one's hometown for one of a stranger's hometown through the mail. Special albums could be purchased that were designed specifically to hold and show off an assembled postcard collection. Before 1900, the use and collecting of postcards in the United States was still very new, and after 1960, their wide use was on the decline.

The images found on old postcards from this time period tend to be more stylized and idealistic than what can be seen in actual photographs.

The images we find on postcards offer, for the most part, scenes of happy and relaxed times that reflect a carefree and genteel atmosphere. We will not see pollution in the water, trash in the street, or rust and peeling paint on the side of a boat. Extra sunny skies, billowing, blue clouds, soft textures, and calm waters overwhelmingly prevail. In the 1940s it was very common to have unsightly objects such as telephone wires, etc, completely airbrushed out of the scene. Yet, with all of that said, postcards offer a tremendously important archive of visual and historical information. The subject matter found on postcards is almost endless. Many times, a postcard view is all that remains, or in other cases, all that there ever was to document an event, a place, a boat, a pier, a building, etc.

Many postcards exist today because they were considered effective promotional tools in their day. It was often a picture postcard that triggered one to think, "I want to be there" or, "I want to do that." The steamboat companies in the Chesapeake Bay region widely used postcards as a method to promote their vessels as a preferred mode of travel. Postcards would be found for sale in the lobby of a resort hotel in the hope that vacationers would take them home and show them off to others or to remind the vacationer of what a good time they had had last summer. Postcards were the perfect souvenir for both the extended vacationer or for the one day, turn around excursionist. Postcards were affordable, transportable, they could be used to send a short message economically through the mail, and again, they had great value in the memories they helped one preserve.

Embossed, shell bordered postcard showing the Old Point Comfort Lighthouse at Fort Monroe, Virginia. Circa 1907-12; $20

There are three distinct types of postcards that are collected: "views," "holidays and greetings," and "topics." Views, also referred to as "local views," are postcards that show scenes of places. A postcard showing the main street of a small town is a good example of a "view" postcard. "Holidays and greetings," however, are purely artistic representations. A typical holiday postcard might be an artist's representation of Santa Claus coming down the chimney on Christmas day, or Uncle Sam waving a flag on July 4th. A typical greeting postcard would be the happy birthday postcard. Topics are just that—topical. A topical collector may collect postcards showing a certain type of animal, for instance dogs, or, perhaps, just Collies. Someone may collect just covered bridges, or just postcards showing fire engines.

Perhaps no subject is discussed more frequently in the world of postcard collecting than that of how to date a postcard. True, at times it can be tricky, and dating any early postcard to its exact year of manufacture is hard indeed. However, once one has a basic understanding of the different styles of postcards and knows the time frame for each style, the process is relatively straightforward. Fortunately, too, many postcards were sent through the mail, and having a postmark date usually leaves little doubt as to the age of a postcard. Many times, however, the postmark date is unreadable or missing. It is helpful to have a basic understanding of postal history. The types of postmarks and cancellations applied to correspondence have changed over time and the subject is well documented. Oftentimes, the image itself helps in the dating of the postcard. Among other things, certain styles of dress or the type of street lighting can be keys to the dating of postcards.

Postcards had already gained wide accep-

tance in Europe by the time they were beginning to be used in the United States. On May 19, 1898, the U.S. Congress granted permission for the private printing and publishing of postcards. These early postcards were required to have the inscription, "Private Mailing Card – Authorized by an Act of Congress" printed on their back side. Private mailing postcards were in general use from 1898 to 1901. The back of the card could only be used for writing the recipient's address. Any message had to be put on the front side. This meant squeezing a short message, at best, in the border area surrounding the picture on the front. I have seen examples where instead of using the border, the sender simply wrote right over the picture. Sometimes the message

added to the front side has been so artistically done that it adds significantly to the value of a postcard. If the handwritten message is sloppy and distracting, it will lessen the value of the postcard.

New regulations became effective on December 24, 1901. After that date, all that was required to be printed on the back side was "Post Card." We call these "Undivided Back" postcards. Undivided Back postcards were in general use from 1901 until March 1907. These again, as the name implies, have Undivided Backs and the back side was for the address only. Any message that the sender wanted to add had to be written on the front where the picture was.

The large steamboat wharf at Old Point Comfort, Virginia was a scene of constant activity. Postmarked 1901; $15

5

On March 1, 1907, a new style of postcard was approved for use by the post office. Already allowed in Europe, now in the United States a message could be put on the back of a postcard. The resulting postcards of this era –1907 to 1915– are known as "Divided Back" postcards. On these postcards, we see a line printed down the middle of the back of the card. To the left of this line is the space for a message. The address was written on the right side of the line. The standard style on the front of the postcard was a glossy chromolithographic image that filled its entire front. This resulted in postcards with more detail and color.

The next distinct style of postcard to arrive on the scene was the "White Border" postcard. These started to appear around 1915, and were being produced until the early 1930s. They are easily recognizable by a white border around the postcard image.

It was not unusual to see as many as three large steamships docked at the same time at the Old Point Comfort, Virginia steamboat wharf. Circa 1920s; $5

STEAMBOAT LANDING AND PIER, AT NIGHT, OLD POINT COMFORT, VA.

57130

Developed in the mid 1930s, the linen postcard was an offshoot of the new printing processes of the time. A linen postcard gets its name from the high rag content and textured finish of the paper on which it was printed. The finish actually looks and feels linen-like. Linen postcards are recognizable by their highly stylized, almost utopian-like art work and the use of brilliant ink colors. Although the design process for many a linen postcard started with a client's photograph, it often ended with an artist's concept of an ideal reality. Anything unsightly or distracting was airbrushed out of the picture. Anything that would add to the visual effectiveness of a postcard was airbrushed in. Linen postcards were popular all through the 1940s and into the early 1950s.

Photochrome postcards, also known as simply chrome postcards, are easily distinguishable because of their photographic quality. They are generally well composed, sharply focused, full color scenes with great detail. By the mid 1950s, they had all but replaced the linen postcard, and were the standard through the 1960s.

Real photo postcards are postcards made from the negatives of actual photographs. Typically, they were not a product of mass production. Oftentimes, only one or two copies were made. With a camera, a few inexpensive chemicals, and a dark room, anyone could make a real photo postcard. In 1902 Kodak began selling photo paper with preprinted "POST CARD" on the back side. The paper also had a stamp box in the upper right corner where the type of photo paper was identified. It became the norm for manufacturers of postcard photo paper to identify the name of their product in the stamp box area. One of the first photo postcard papers was "azo." However, the style of the name "azo" in the stamp box area changed over time. Therefore, it is still possible to date real photo postcards made with azo paper fairly accurately even though the paper was used until the early 1940s. Another popular photo paper used to make real photo postcards was "EKC." This photo paper was in use from around 1939 to 1950. "DOPS" was the name of a photo paper used from around 1925 to 1942. Photo paper labeled with the name "Kodak" in the stamp box was not introduced until 1950.

How much is it worth? Is it rare? Everybody seems to want to know. With postcards, the primary factor that determines the price is demand. Second after demand is condition. A rare postcard that is in great demand and is in nice condition will be worth the most. A rare postcard with no demand is worth very little. A postcard in great demand but with major condition problems will have only moderate value to the collector. Demand can and does change. Prices go up and down as collectors enter and exit the marketplace. Demand for local-view postcards is generally the highest when they

are being offered to collectors in the area which the cards depict. Postcards of California being offered for sale to Maryland collectors will not be in big demand.

When it comes to pricing postcards, there is no substitute for experience. It is a skill learned by doing. Correct pricing is learned by handling lots of postcards over a long period of time. By direct interaction with the collectors, one learns the demand (or the market, as I like to say) for postcards. By handling the material, one learns what is common, scarce, rare, and truly rare. Novice sellers tend to price postcards either too high or too low. They either have their postcards priced at a level where they will keep them for a long time or at such a low level that a knowledgeable dealer will come along and buy everything. Older is not always better. Many postcards from the 1940s and 1950s are now bringing better prices than those from the earlier years. Some of the better postcards from these later years are also harder to find than their earlier counterparts.

The publishing of postcards in the Chesapeake Bay region tended to be a localized undertaking. This mirrored the trend of postcard publishing across the United States in the early and first half of the twentieth century. Oftentimes, it was an enterprising individual, or the local druggist or stationer who would produce a series of postcards of their hometown. Exceptions were always to be had. I. & M. Ottenheimer of Baltimore, Maryland published postcards of the entire Chesapeake Bay region. Their first postcards were black and white, Undivided Back views of the 1905 era. Louis Kaufmann & Sons, also of Baltimore, soon followed and became a prolific postcard publisher throughout the Bay, as well as other areas. Kaufmann's earliest cards are divided back, color postcards of the 1908 era. There were many smaller, more localized publishers of postcards. William Tutty published postcards exclusively of Chesapeake Beach, Maryland. Henry Rinn published postcards of Betterton, Tolchester Beach, and Baltimore, Maryland exclusively. George W. Jones published postcards of Annapolis, Maryland and lower Anne Arundel County. Caruthers & Coakley published postcards of Colonial Beach, Virginia. W. T. Wise, published postcards of Onancock, Virginia. Indeed, there were many other publishers of Chesapeake Bay area postcards. Many postcards have no publisher information at all listed on them.

Old Bay Line Pier, Baltimore, Md.

THE BALTIMORE STEAM PACKET CO.
LEAVES BALTIMORE EVERY WEEK DAY AT 6.30 P. M.
FOR OLD POINT, NORFOLK AND PORTSMOUTH.

The Baltimore terminal of the Old Bay Line was located at Pier 10, Light Street. Circa 1907-12; $8

# HISTORY OF THE CHESAPEAKE BAY

The Chesapeake Bay is considered the largest estuary (an area where fresh and salt water meet) in the world. The Bay is bounded by the state of Maryland in its northern half, and by the state of Virginia in its southern half. The head of the Chesapeake Bay is generally considered to be at the junction where the Susquehanna River meets the Bay at the towns of Havre de Grace and Perryville, Maryland. The mouth of the Bay is bounded by Cape Charles to its north and Cape Henry to its south, and is at a point where the Bay meets the Atlantic Ocean. The distance between the head of the Bay and its mouth is approximately 189 miles when measured in a general north – south direction. The Chesapeake Bay is at its narrowest point near Annapolis, where it is about four miles wide. It is its widest off the mouth of the Potomac River, being approximately thirty miles wide at that point. The Chesapeake Bay is fed by over 150 rivers and streams.

At the beginning of the twentieth century and the dawn of the postcard era, the Chesapeake Bay was one big seafood harvesting and production factory, a booming natural playground and an important north – south nautical transportation route. These industries, the harvesting and production of seafood, recreation, and transportation, were inextricably linked to one another and each was dependent upon the success of the others for its survival.

With its generally shallow shorelines and sandy bottom, the Bay was an ideal location for a beach. Numerous beaches dotted the map from one end of the Chesapeake Bay to the other. The larger beaches were located directly on the Bay and along its major rivers. Yet, any body of water that somehow splintered off from the Bay's main stream was a candidate for, and often did host a beach. The larger beaches were accessible by both car and steamboat, and sometimes by train or trolley. A fair number of the smaller beaches were serviced by regular excursion boat traffic, but primarily they were "drive to" destinations. Their expansive dirt parking lots overflowed daily during the summer months. No matter its size, each beach was known by, and seemed to take on its own character. Some beaches were known for their rough and tumble crowd, the majority for their family atmosphere. A full support system from hotels to amusements and social activities was available at the larger beaches. Except for a snack bar and an unassuming bath house, you were basically on your own at a small beach.

Travel and transportation was by steamboat. Various specialty steamboat lines existed to serve the different parts and the different needs that existed on the Chesapeake Bay. The Baltimore Steam Packet Company, also known as the Old Bay Line, began steamboat service on the Bay in 1840. For the traveler on one of their night boats, the time passed quickly between the big city ports of Baltimore and Norfolk. While making the trip, one could dine on Broiled Spanish Mackerel with Corn Cakes, Fried Select Oysters with Bacon or Roast Young Maryland Turkey with Dressing. From the open air deck one could watch the sun go down and the moon rise over a constantly changing tidewater panorama. The aft saloon was popular with those seeking a comfortable chair and a good book. Gentlemen gathered around the fireplace in the smoking room. Staterooms had double beds with deep mattresses, dressing tables, and private baths. The nightly 6:30 P.M. departure of the Old Bay Line boat at Baltimore, blowing its whistle, backing and turning out of its berth at Pier 10 on Light Street, was such a routine and expected event that few witnessing it would give it any more than a business as usual, passing thought.

The Baltimore and Philadelphia Steamboat Company, otherwise known as the Ericsson Line, offered passage to and from Philadelphia by way of the Chesapeake and Delaware Canal. Due to the constraints in the width of the canal before it was enlarged in 1927, the company's vessels up to that time had all been especially built to traverse it. They had narrower than normal beams and were all rear propeller driven. This gave their vessels a slim and sleek appearance. They were easily distinguished from other craft on the Bay.

The excursion steamer *S.S. Dixie* navigating the Chesapeake Bay between Baltimore and Seaside Park, Maryland. Circa 1936-41; $15

For those with less of a need to get to some specific place, but with more of a need to have some fun, the daytime and nighttime excursion boats were the answer. Throughout the 1930s and the early 1940s, the Wilson Line operated daily summertime excursions from Baltimore down the Bay to Seaside Park. Typically, the boat left the company's dock at Pier 8, Light Street at 9 A.M. and arrived at the Park several hours later. The boat would leave the park at 4 P.M. This gave the passengers just enough time to splash their feet in the Chesapeake, enjoy a picnic grove lunch, and take a dip in the large swimming pool. The Wilson Line also offered nightly two-hour cruises. The boat would leave Baltimore at 8:30 P.M. Touted as an opportunity to "Dance in the Moonlight," the boat had a large dance floor and the music was provided by a small orchestra.

Ever so popular with Baltimoreans were the boat rides to Tolchester Beach. Tolchester was a leisurely two-hour ride across the Bay via excursion boat. One could catch the boat several times each day at the Tolchester Lines dock on Light Street. Tolchester was a popular destination for company outings and church picnics. It was the ideal place to spend the day with the family. As the boat pulled up to the large Tolchester Pier, children would jockey for positions so as to be the first off the boat. They would run down the pier and up the hill to the picnic groves and grab what they thought was the best picnic table for mom and dad. Tolchester overlooked the wide expanse of the Bay. There were amusement park rides, games of chance and of course, salt water bathing. A little, coal fired steam engine nicknamed Jumbo pulled several open air cars as it chugged along at eight miles per hour on an oval track that included a bridge and a tunnel. There was a hotel and a restaurant, famous for its fresh vegetables from local farms and Chesapeake Bay seafood meals cooked to perfection.

A 1930s view of the excursion steamer *Tolchester* on the way to Tolchester Beach, Maryland. Circa 1933-36; $30

Big New Steel Excursion Steamer
**"TOLCHESTER"**
Plying between Baltimore, Md. and Tolchester Beach — the Beautiful Excursion Resort — Fine Salt Water Bathing — Delicious Meals
Tolchester Co., Pier 16 Light St., Baltimore, Md.

Before the completion of the Chesapeake Bay Bridge, the Eastern Shore of Maryland was not as easily accessible. Vehicular traffic had to be shuffled across the Bay via car ferries. The Chesapeake Bay Ferry System maintained a fleet of five vessels and operated ferry service between Sandy Point on the Annapolis side and Matapeake at Kent Island on the Eastern Shore. The-four-and-one-half mile crossing took a half hour. It was just enough time to grab a bite to eat in the snack bar and to take a stroll around the upper deck of the ferry boat. The ferry service came to an abrupt end on July 30, 1952, the day the Chesapeake Bay Bridge opened. The *Governor Herbert R O'Connor*, newest vessel of the fleet, was chosen to make the final crossing. She departed the Matapeake terminal at 5:30 P.M. On board were Governor McKeldin and B. Frank Sherman, general manager of the ferry system. The *O'Connor* pulled into the Sandy Point terminal at 5:55 P.M. The governor quickly departed and made his way up to the toll booth area of the new bridge. The driver of the car first in line had been waiting two days for the privilege of being the first to cross the bridge. Photos of the driver were taken as he paid his fare and traffic started to roll across the bridge. The whistle of the *O'Connor* let out a long blow in tribute to the new bridge. It is still possible to discern the remains of the old ferry boat slips if one looks off to the right after leaving the toll booth at Sandy Point.

The Kiptopeke Beach – Little Creek Ferries, operated by the Virginia Ferry Corporation, predecessor to the Chesapeake Bay Bridge Tunnel, offered car ferry service across the mouth of the Chesapeake. As the name implies, service was between Little Creek, Virginia (Norfolk) to the south and Kiptopeke Beach, Virginia (Cape Charles) to the north. The twenty-one mile crossing took one hour and twenty-five minutes. One

of the company's old promotional brochures assured the motorist: "You're sure to drive off refreshed – with a memory of a pleasant Chesapeake Bay cruise." In the mid 1950s, the ferry service was operating with a fleet of five ships making twenty-two round trips daily. Several years later, two additional vessels were added and the ferry service was operating around the clock at full capacity. Those riding the ferry in its last years watched the daily progress being made on the Chesapeake Bay Bridge Tunnel. The structure was completed in 1964 and with its opening, the days of car ferry service across the Chesapeake Bay became history.

The commercial seafood industry in the Chesapeake Bay region includes the harvesting and processing of oysters, crabs, and fish. The Eastern American, or Native Oyster, as it is called on the bay, is primarily found at a water depth of eight to twenty-five feet. Traditionally the harvesting of oysters was done during the "R" months, meaning any month that had an "R" in its spelling, or September to April.

Watermen harvest oysters by either dredging or tonging. Dredging involves dragging a metal frame with a net over the bottom of the Bay. This scraping over an oyster bar loosens the oysters and they are deposited in the net. The dredge is then raised to the surface and the oysters are culled (sorted) out. Undersized oysters, and whatever else came up in the net, are then deposited back in the water. The dredging of oysters has long been restricted to sailing craft only.

Hand tongs are a long scissors-like tool varying in length from twenty-four to thirty feet in length. The two shafts are made out of wood, and at the end of each shaft is a metal rake head with steel teeth. The tonger stabilizes himself on the side of the boat, lowers the tongs to the bottom and maneuvers them around in an

open scissors fashion. When he feels that he has some oysters, he pulls the two shafts together and nips the oysters from the bottom. Careful to keep the shafts together, he raises the tongs, hand over hand, until he reaches the contents of the rakes, which he then drops onto a culling board for sorting.

An alternative to hand tongs is the mechanized Patent Tongs. These have a scissors-like claw which is designed to open as it is lowered to the Bay's bottom and to close upon being raised. The claw is attached to a steel cable and is raised and lowered by a machine powered winch.

The end of the oystering season in April ushers in the beginning of the crabbing season in May. However, blue crabs don't normally become active or appear in any numbers that would make it profitable to pursue them until the end of May. The crabbing season continues throughout the warm months and ends around mid October. Commercial crabbing is generally done by either using crab pots or with the use of a trot line.

A Chesapeake Bay area invention of the 1920s, the crab pot is an enclosed framework of galvanized chicken wire that measures two feet by two feet by two feet . It is divided into two sections: the bottom half, which holds the bait in an enclosed chamber of chicken wire, and the top section, which holds the captured crabs. The crab pot works like this: in the bottom half are two to four funnel shaped openings made of chicken wire which allow the crab access. The crab works its way down a funnel in an attempt to reach the bait. Once the crab finds its way through the funnel, it is trapped. Sensing that it is trapped, and finding it impossible to re-enter the funnel from its narrow end, the crab, by nature, swims upwards. Another funnel awaits the crab. The crab meanders down that funnel and finds itself in the upper portion or the holding area of the trap. Unable to enter the funnel from the narrow end, the crab is joined by other crabs and awaits its fate.

The preferred bait for crab pots is salted eel or fish parts. In the evening, the crabber will place a good number of pots in water that is approximately eight to fifteen feet deep and let them sit (soak) on the bottom overnight. Each pot is attached to a line with a distinctive float so that the crabber knows which pots are his. The next day he locates his pots and, one by one, hauls them to the surface. A trap door in the top of each pot facilitates the removal of the crabs. The bait chamber of each pot gets examined, and bait is either added or replaced. Minor repairs are also done to any damaged pots. After each pot has been emptied, had its bait tended to, and passed inspection, it gets lowered back to the bottom for more crabs to find.

Commercial crabbers also use a trot line to catch (dip) crabs in an assembly line fashion. In its most simple form, a trot line is a long line parlayed out in a straight line across the bottom of the water. At each end are heavy weights to hold it on the bottom in a relatively taut position. Separate lines secured to each end of the trot line rise to the surface and are kept there by floats. The floats allow the crabber to easily locate each end of the trot line and to show the length of the trot line. At regular intervals of between two to six feet, bait is secured with slip knots to the trot line. Salted eel is the preferred bait for a trot line. After the trot line has been submerged on the bottom for some time, the crabber brings his boat up to one of the floats. He slowly brings the end of the trot line to the surface. Then he loops the trot line onto the top of a small revolving wheel with guides attached to a board extending perpendicularly from the side of the boat two or three feet. He slowly runs his boat along the length of the trot line. The crabs feasting on the bait don't seem to care or are unaware that they are being drawn to the surface as the line rolls over the wheel. The crabs are caught with the dip net just as they reach the surface.

The Chesapeake Bay is populated with over two hundred species of fish. The most desirable catch from the standpoint of commercial fishing is the striped bass, herring, shad, bluefish, perch, spot, croaker, and menhaden. The states of Maryland and Virginia have many rules and regulations that distinguish what is commercial fishing from what is recreational sport fishing. However, the most telling are the methods used to catch fish. The sport fisherman uses a rod and reel, with a baited hook. He catches his fish one at a time. The commercial fisherman employs nets to harvest his catch. A variety of net types are used on the Bay, the use of which is determined by location and type of fish being sought.

The pound net is a fixed fish trap consisting of netting attached to poles that have been driven into the Bay's bottom. The trap has three distinct parts: the leader, the heart, and the pound, also called the crib. The leader is a long, straight net which stops the fish and diverts them into the heart. The fish are gathered in the heart which is funnel shaped at one end. The fish find their way through this funnel and are then trapped in the pound. The fish are scooped out of the pound with a dip net. A gill net works in a different fashion, the difference being that the netting is of a size and the holes of a dimension that cause fish to get entangled in it. There are several variations of the gill net. Fixed gill nets are set by way of stakes and anchors. Drift gill nets are used in deeper water and are put over the side of boats. The bottom part of the drift net is weighted to hold the gill net in an up and down position. A gill net acts like a curtain in the water. As fish swim into the netting, their heads are able to pass through, but the net catches the fish behind the gills, hence the name gill net. Smaller fish sometimes get further through the netting, but get snagged in their midsection.

Menhaden are fish that swim in large schools near the surface of the water. The fish are not caught for food. Instead, they are used as a bait fish and the oil processed from the fish is used in the manufacture of a variety of products from ink to plastics. The harvesting of Menhaden is done in the Virginia part of the Bay with a purse seine. A purse seine is a large net that is used to catch the fish. When a school of Menhaden is spotted, the fishing vessel quickly lets out the purse seine as it encircles the school of fish. Once the boat has the school of fish encircled with the net, the net is then pursed; in other words, the bottom part of the net is drawn tightly together, trapping the fish inside. The net with its catch of fish is then hauled onto the fishing vessel.

## ABOUT THE POSTCARDS AND THEIR VALUES

The postcards used to illustrate this book are from the author's personal collection. The value amount assigned to each postcard is an estimate only. It reflects what one could normally expect to pay when purchasing a comparable postcard in clean and collectible condition. Postcards with bent corners, creases, or other types of damage bring lower prices. Superb examples will always command premium prices. The pricing of postcards is very subjective, varying from dealer to dealer. A dealer's price for a postcard is determined by that dealer's idea of desirability, rarity, and what the market will bear.

Postcards are wonderful and unique pieces of history that we can hold in our hands. Every postcard has a story to tell. As a group, the postcards in this book tell the story of an earlier time on the Chesapeake Bay. It has often been said that we cannot understand where we are going unless we know where we have already been. Here, in this book, is an open window to the Chesapeake Bay's past.

Swimming and boating were popular summertime activities at the Faulkner House in Fairbank, Maryland. Circa 1907-12; $15

Faulkner House, Fairbank, Md.

## BAY SHORE PARK, MARYLAND

"For a good, salt air breeze, ocean bath, seafood supper, take the trolley to Bay Shore Park." So read the headline in the August 31, 1912 edition of "Trolley News," a handout, giveaway-type publication of the United Railways and Electric Co., which operated trolley service around Baltimore at the time. The "Ocean Bath" exaltation may have been a stretch, but Bay Shore Park did have much to offer those that took the short trip from downtown Baltimore to the amusement park and beach located on the Bay, near North Point. There was a rickety, wooden roller coaster, a miniature railroad train, a penny arcade, and a shooting gallery. A Maryland style seafood supper could be enjoyed in the dining room for seventy-five cents. There was a 1000-foot pier which afforded one a panoramic view of the amusement park and the Bay. Bathing was the park's main attraction, and there was a large bathing pavilion where valuables could be checked and ladies' and mens' bathing suits could be rented. Bathers normally had to wait in line for the toboggan water slide which propelled them down a steep incline and then deposited them with a big splash in the briny deep. The sea swing was a merry-go-round of sorts that swung, swirled, and plunged one into the water. From bowling alleys for the adults to a merry-

go-round for the young ones, Bay Shore Park had it all. And yes, just like the headline said, on a good clear day, a salt air breeze filtered through the park from offshore. Bay Shore Park closed in 1947. When it was operational, it was typical of many of the other amusement parks and bathing beaches which dotted the shores of the Chesapeake Bay.

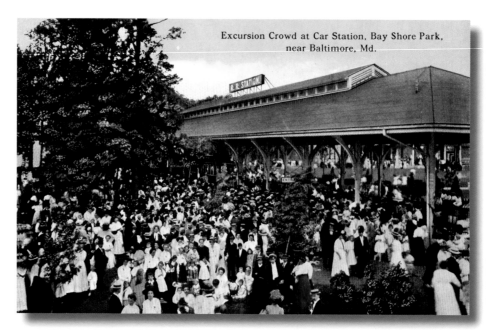

Excursion Crowd at Car Station, Bay Shore Park, near Baltimore, Md.

A huge crowd at the trolley car station, Bay Shore Park, near Baltimore, Maryland. Circa 1907-12; $15

A bird's eye view of Bay Shore Park, near Baltimore, Maryland. The one thousand foot concrete pier was clearly a popular place to be. Circa 1907-12; $10

The moving picture pavilion at Bay Shore Park, Maryland. Circa 1904-07; $12

The band stand and fountain were surrounded by concrete walkways and well manicured lawns at Bay Shore Park. Circa 1904-07; $10

The pavilion at Bay Shore Park, near Baltimore, Maryland. Circa 1920s; $7

"Part of Midway," Bay Shore Park, Baltimore, Md.

Part of the midway at Bay Shore Park, Maryland.
The handwritten message on the backside reads:
"Just got off the rocket and feel sick as a dog.
Love, Mary." Postmarked 1946; $15

WATER SWING AT BAY SHORE PARK

The beach and water swing at Bay Shore Park,
Maryland. Circa 1930s; $20

DIVING PLATFORM AT BAY SHORE PARK

The diving platform at Bay Shore Park,
Maryland. Circa 1930s; $20

# TOLCHESTER BEACH, MARYLAND

Tolchester Beach was an amusement park, bathing beach, and picnic area located slightly north and across the Bay from Bay Shore Park. By excursion steamer from Baltimore, it was a two-hour, twenty-seven-mile trip. Its roots as a resort destination dated back to 1877. A 1943 brochure informs the excursionist that they will find an "Excellent sandy beach, boating, dancing, fishing, riding horses, roller skating rink, illuminated baseball diamond, complete and up-to-date amusement park." The same brochure describes a week-long stay at the Hotel Tolchester for two with meals included, cost only $42.00. Tolchester Beach was proclaimed by its owners to be the "Most popular Bathing Beach on Chesapeake Bay." Tolchester Beach closed in 1962; the site of the old beach is now occupied by a marina.

Steamer *Louise* landing excursionists at Tolchester Beach, Maryland. Circa 1907-12; $10

Steamer *Louise* on her way across the Chesapeake Bay to Tolchester Beach, Maryland. Circa 1907-12; $30

The new arch entrance at Tolchester Beach, Maryland. Circa 1907-12; $8

The Whirl-Pool Dips at Tolchester Beach,
Maryland. Postmarked 1930; $15

The souvenir stand at Tolchester Beach. The large sign
on the roof reads: "Souvenirs of all kinds, postcards
and shells, views of Tolchester for sale here." Postmarked 1910; $20

The Tickler was one of the popular rides at Tolchester
Beach. Several individuals would sit together in a round,
saucer shaped tub on coaster wheels. After being hauled
up an incline, the saucer would be propelled downward by
gravity and speed through a maze of track. All the while its
occupants would be bounced and tossed about in the tub
as it spun around, seemingly out of control, and bounced
off cushioned railings. Postmarked 1911; $20

The goat track at Tolchester Beach, Maryland. Postmarked 1932; $10

The hotel at Tolchester Beach sat up on a bluff over-looking the Chesapeake Bay. Circa 1940s; $15

The bathing beach at Tolchester Beach, Maryland. Circa 1910-15; $10

Bathing scene at Tolchester Beach, Maryland. Circa 1940s; $15

A side view of the hotel at Tolchester Beach, Maryland. Circa 1940s; $15

The miniature train ride was a hit with adults as well as children at Tolchester Beach. Postmarked 1912; $20

# BETTERTON BEACH, MARYLAND

Betterton is located in Kent County, Maryland, near the mouth of the Sassafras River. From the many old postcards that have survived, it can be seen that Betterton was a very popular destination for the excursionist. Betterton had several piers and was a stop for the steamers of both the Tolchester Steamboat Company and the Ericsson Line. In the mid 1940s, the Wilson Line began running a daily three-hour cruise from Baltimore down the Patapsco River and up and across the Chesapeake Bay to Betterton with their excursion boat, the *Bay Belle*. Betterton's two most popular hotels were the Rigbie, which sat on a high bluff overlooking the beach, and the Chesapeake Hotel, which sat almost directly on the beach. The Chesapeake Hotel was a five story frame structure with wrap around porches on its first two levels, and had lots of benches for watching the bathers. The Emerson, Hotel Betterton, and Owens Cottage were also popular hotels at Betterton.

Daily dozen health exercises on the beach, Betterton, Maryland. Postmarked 1923; $20

The Ericsson Line steamer at the end of the Ericsson Line Pier, Betterton, Maryland. Postmarked 1923; $15

Automobile square and Chesapeake Hotel at Betterton Beach, Maryland. Circa 1916-25; $15

21

Parking Space Foot of Chesapeake Ave. showing Hotel Rigbie, Betterton, Md.

21609

Parking lot at the foot of Chesapeake Avenue, Betterton, Maryland. Postmarked 1936; $15

BETTERTON, MD.
PRICE COTTAGE

PRICE COTTAGE

Arrive
Safe.
Very nice
place
Yours
Sister
Louise

The Price Cottage at Betterton, Maryland. Postmarked 1906; $15

9.

The Emerson, Betterton, Md.

THE EMERSON

Guests enjoying the front lawn of the Emerson at Betterton Beach, Maryland. Postmarked 1908; $15

Hotel Rigbie sat up on a bluff overlooking the pier and Bay at Betterton Beach. The handwritten message on the backside reads: "We are at the hotel pictured on the front. It is a lovely place. We are in the hotel addressing our cards." Postmarked 1943; $15

HOTEL RIGBIE AND PIER, BETTERTON, MD.

The Hotel Rigbie had plenty of shade trees and a wraparound porch for fresh air and relaxation. Circa 1907-12; $15

HOTEL RIGBIE. BETTERTON, Md.

## Cottage Grove Park and Fairview Beach, Maryland

A short distance down the Patapsco River from Baltimore in Anne Arundel County is Rock Creek. Just inside the creek, on its southeast side, was located Fairview Beach. A short distance up the creek and on its opposite side stood Cottage Grove, which was also known as Heintzeman's. Both Fairview and Cottage Grove were popular daytime pleasure parks. They offered the visitor a bathing beach, picnic groves, and covered pavilions. Fairview Beach had a modest style, turn-of-the-century hotel, a carousel, and a penny arcade with larger than life cutouts of toy soldiers guarding each side of its entrance. The owners of Cottage Grove Park proclaimed their park to be: "Maryland's finest seashore picnic park," offering "acres of C-O-O-L shady groves and playgrounds on Chesapeake Bay waters." However, taking up most of the real estate at the park was its large dirt parking lot which was filled to capacity on summer weekends. The paid admissions at Cottage Grove for the summer of 1947 came to 21,539, an impressive number for the time.

Cottage Grove Park

"Maryland's Finest Bathing and Amusement Resort"

Plan Your Outing for "Cotta...

Cottage Grove Beach on Rock Creek was: "Fun for Everybody." Circa 1950s; $8

Cocktail Lounge and Bar
COTTAGE GROVE BEACH

Spacious Marine Dining Room
COTTAGE GROVE BEACH

The spacious marine dining room and cocktail lounge at Colonial Beach, Maryland. Circa 1940s; $8

Bath Houses and Beach at Fairview Beach

The bath houses and beach at Fairview Beach, Maryland. The handwritten message on the backside reads: "You should be here to have a good time." Postmarked 1936; $20

24

Beginning in 1938, the steamer *Mohawk* transported excursionists from Baltimore to Fairview Beach, Maryland. Circa 1938; $15

Steamer "Mohawk" at Fairview Pier

Carousel & Penny Arcade at Fairview Beach, Md.

The carousel and penny arcade at Fairview Beach, Maryland. Circa 1930s; $25

Fair View on the Patapsco, Baltimore, Md.

A pleasure boat at Fairview Beach, near Baltimore, Maryland. Circa 1907-12; $8

# CHESAPEAKE BEACH, MARYLAND

In the early 1890s, a group of investors envisioned a lavish and expansive resort on the shores of the Chesapeake Bay. The resort would be serviced by its own railway from Washington, DC. Thousands would flock to their resort from far and wide. A pleasant setting on the bay, which would allow for the building of the railway in a nearly straight line from the city, was chosen. The new resort was to be called Chesapeake Beach. From the start, the grandiose plans for the railway and resort lacked proper planning, and budget problems plagued the project. Creditors soon loomed over the company. The uncompleted railway and resort went into receivership and ended up being sold to new investors. Principal amongst the new investors was Otto Mears, a railroad builder from Colorado. Delays, financial woes, and internal bickering haunted the new company. Still, Mears managed to see the railway to completion and a much more modest, scaled back version of the resort opened to the public in June of 1900. Advertisements announcing its opening read: "Created at a cost of one million dollars by the men who made Colorado famous." The new boardwalk was said to be a mile long. It was built out over the water and ran parallel to the shore line. On the boardwalk a carousel, band shell, and a variety of other amusements were located.

For years, Chesapeake Beach was popular with those from Washington and Baltimore. Yet the resort never seemed to make a profit. The high cost of maintaining the railway, the boardwalk, steamboat pier, and employee payroll ate up the revenue generated. The elaborate Dentzel carousel burned in 1926. By the end of the 1920s, the boardwalk was in such disrepair that the only solution was to demolish it and move its attractions to the shore. In 1930, the revamped amusement park was renamed "Seaside Park." A miniature train began operating on the long steamboat pier. It was kept busy hauling steamboat passengers from one end of the pier to the other. Train service to the park ended in 1935 because so few were riding the railway by that time. In 1948, slot machines were legalized in Calvert County. Gambling and the post war boom breathed new life into the amusement park. The park by then had been renamed Chesapeake Beach Park. Crowds would arrive by auto on Friday and Saturday nights. They came for the big bands, the dancing, the drinking, and to drop nickels into the "one-armed bandits." When slot machines were outlawed in 1968, the crowds disappeared. The amusement park closed for good at the end of the 1972 season.

The arrival of the steamer *Dreamland* at Chesapeake Beach, Maryland. Dated 1909; $20

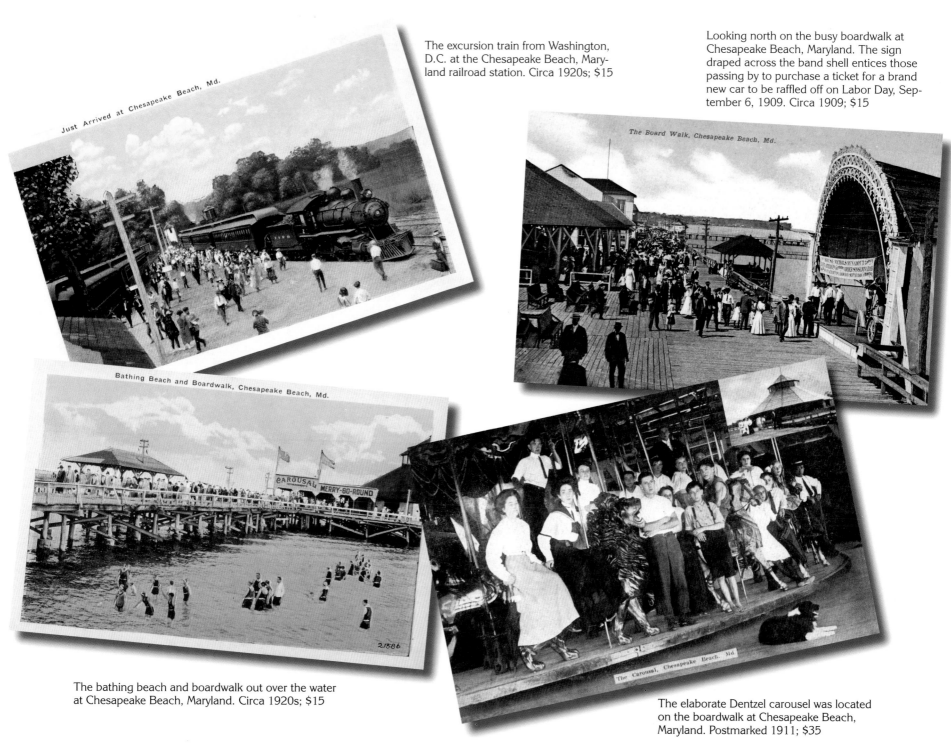

The excursion train from Washington, D.C. at the Chesapeake Beach, Maryland railroad station. Circa 1920s; $15

Looking north on the busy boardwalk at Chesapeake Beach, Maryland. The sign draped across the band shell entices those passing by to purchase a ticket for a brand new car to be raffled off on Labor Day, September 6, 1909. Circa 1909; $15

Just Arrived at Chesapeake Beach, Md.

The Board Walk, Chesapeake Beach, Md.

Bathing Beach and Boardwalk, Chesapeake Beach, Md.

CAROUSAL MERRY-GO-ROUND

21586

The Carousal, Chesapeake Beach, Md.

The bathing beach and boardwalk out over the water at Chesapeake Beach, Maryland. Circa 1920s; $15

The elaborate Dentzel carousel was located on the boardwalk at Chesapeake Beach, Maryland. Postmarked 1911; $35

The Oyster and Crab House was located on the boardwalk at Chesapeake Beach, Maryland. Postmarked 1913; $25

Looking south down the boardwalk at Chesapeake Beach, Maryland. Circa 1907-12; $20

The large roller coaster called the Great Derby sat out over the water at Chesapeake Beach. It was certainly an attraction that had many lookers, as this postcard attests to. Circa 1907-12; $30

The dancing pavilion on the boardwalk at Chesapeake Beach. The handwritten message on the backside reads: "We are here for the day. You ought to see us dancing." Postmarked 1909; $15

The scenic railway on the boardwalk at Chesapeake Beach, Maryland. Postmarked 1909; $15

A view of the long steamboat pier at Seaside Park, Maryland. The excursion boat is barely visible at the end of the pier. To the left is the open passenger car which was pulled from one end of the pier to the other by the miniature railroad engine. Postmarked 1940; $25

The swimming pool at Seaside Park, Maryland. Postmarked 1931; $15

The dance hall at Seaside Park, Maryland. Circa 1930s; $25

The ballroom entrance at Seaside Park, Maryland. Circa 1930s; $25

The miniature train on the pier at Seaside Park, Maryland. Perhaps one of the best jobs to be had at the park was being the engineer of the miniature train. Circa 1930s; $25

The Wilson Line's steamer *Dixie* docked at the long pier at Seaside Park. Many riders stepped right off the excursion boat and onto the miniature train for the foot saving ride to the park. Circa 1930s; $20

# Colonial Beach, Virginia

Colonial Beach is located in Virginia's Westmoreland County and fronts directly on the southern side of the Potomac River. In the 1890s, a group of investors decided that the area would be an ideal location for a steamboat pier and excursion resort. Soon crowds from Washington, DC were arriving at the resort by steamboat. A boardwalk and hotel were built; other attractions followed. The popularity of the bathing beach is summed up by the sender of a postcard in August 1910, who writes: "A real hot Sunday here, but could not get into the water because the bath house was full." In 1949, when slot machines became legal in Charles County, Maryland, several gambling piers were built jutting out into the Potomac River to get around Virginia's ban on gambling. The boundary of Maryland extended to the low water mark on the Virginia side, meaning the waters of the Potomac were technically a part of Maryland. The fact that Maryland, contrary to Virginia, had a law which allowed liquor by the drink didn't hurt either. Soon throngs were flocking to Colonial Beach and walking out onto the gambling piers to pull the handles of slot machines legally in Maryland waters. One of the gambling and drinking piers, the Reno, was proclaimed by its owners to be: "East Coast's finest amusement pier." The big boom for Colonial Beach came to a bust in 1958 when Maryland amended its slot machine law to forbid slot machines at establishments which couldn't be reached from Maryland soil. The Reno and Monte Carlo piers burned in 1963.

Steamer *St. John's* unloading excursionists at Colonial Beach, Virginia. Circa 1907-12; $20

Proper beach attire, Circa 1909 at Colonial Beach, Virginia. Postmarked 1910; $15

31

Waiting for the excursion boat at Colonial Beach, Virginia. Postmarked 1909; $12

Hats were in fashion on this busy day on the boardwalk at Colonial Beach, Virginia. Postmarked 1906; $20

Crabbing from the pier at Colonial Beach, Virginia. Postmarked 1906; $15

The excursion steamer *Potomac* has arrived at Colonial Beach with a full load of passengers. Postmarked 1945; $10

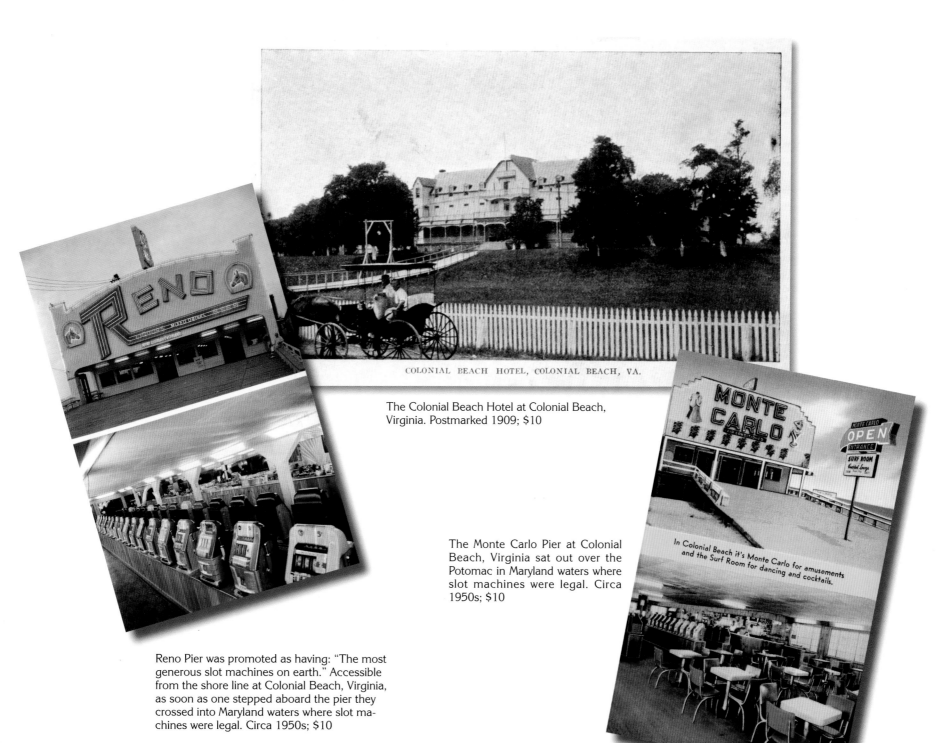

COLONIAL BEACH HOTEL, COLONIAL BEACH, VA.

The Colonial Beach Hotel at Colonial Beach,
Virginia. Postmarked 1909; $10

The Monte Carlo Pier at Colonial
Beach, Virginia sat out over the
Potomac in Maryland waters where
slot machines were legal. Circa
1950s; $10

In Colonial Beach it's Monte Carlo for amusements
and the Surf Room for dancing and cocktails.

Reno Pier was promoted as having: "The most
generous slot machines on earth." Accessible
from the shore line at Colonial Beach, Virginia,
as soon as one stepped aboard the pier they
crossed into Maryland waters where slot machines were legal. Circa 1950s; $10

# BUCKROE BEACH, VIRGINIA

Buckroe Beach is located on the lower peninsula of Virginia and fronts directly on the Chesapeake Bay. It is a short distance from Hampton and Old Point Comfort. As a resort, Buckroe Beach came of age in 1897 when the Buckroe Beach Hotel was constructed. A bath house, amusement park, and dance pavilion soon followed. A circa 1950s brochure promoting Buckroe Beach reads: "Today it is the most popular family amusement park and beach on the Atlantic seaboard. A white sand beach with gentle, rolling Chesapeake Bay waves make[s] Buckroe Beach a vacation paradise." Indeed, during the 1950s, there were many summer weekends when finding a secluded spot on the beach was all but impossible. The amusement park and roller coaster called the "Dips" were closed in 1985.

Passengers getting off the excursion train at Buckroe Beach, Virginia. Circa 1907-12; $15

Arrival of an excursion train from Richmond at Buckroe Beach, Virginia. Circa 1907-12; $15

Buckroe Beach Hotel. The handwritten message on the backside reads: "Spent today at the beach. Had a fine time." Postmarked July 1909; $15

The carousel, ferris wheel, and theater at Buckroe
Beach, Virginia. Postmarked July 1910; $15

Bathers being entertained by a U.S. Army Dirigible flying
over Buckroe Beach, Virginia. Circa 1920s; $15

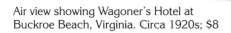

Air view showing Wagoner's Hotel at
Buckroe Beach, Virginia. Circa 1920s; $8

Groves' Inn and bath house at Buckroe
Beach, Virginia. Circa 1930s; $8

# OCEAN VIEW, VIRGINIA

An early, turn-of-the-century brochure describes Ocean View as: "a magnificent stretch of shining, hard white sand with miles of frontage on Chesapeake Bay … the finest and safest bathing beach of any seaside resort." Ocean View was easily reached by streetcar from downtown Norfolk. The Ocean View Hotel was a commanding Victorian frame structure fronting directly on the boardwalk and the Chesapeake Bay. It was wrapped in well cared for green lawns, cemented sidewalks and shaded piazzas. The hotel's central lobby was impressive yet comfortable with large architectural columns and a generous appointment of wicker furniture. At Ocean View was the famous Ocean View Amusement Park, with its many rides and games of chance. Kiddyland was a special area within the amusement park with rides just for children. Some of the attractions at the amusement park were the fun house, a canal of Venice ride, a miniature train, and the sky-ride. One of the best views of Ocean View was from atop the roller coaster called the Skyrocket. The caption on an old 1930s era postcard describes Ocean View in a poetic way.

"A sandy beach with waves so blue,
A thousand bathers – not a few -
A gala crowd – diversions new -
And there you have – Old Ocean
View."

The amusement park closed in 1978.

A view of the manicured lawns and busy sidewalks at Ocean View, Virginia. Circa 1907-12; $15

The Ocean View Hotel and lawn at Ocean View, Virginia. Circa 1916-25; $5

A night view showing the airplane ride and the casino at Ocean View. Postmarked Aug. 1935; $6

The dance hall at Ocean View, Virginia. Circa 1916-25; $10

The Skyrocket roller coaster at Ocean View, Virginia. Circa 1920s; $10

The ferris wheel at the amusement park at Ocean View, Virginia. Circa 1920s; $8

OTHER BEACHES

Ocean View Summer Resort, near Norfolk, Va.

Busy beach scene at Ocean View. The photographer must have taken the picture in the early spring as everyone is dressed warmly and no one is in the water. Circa 1907-12; $10

WHITE STONE BEACH RESORT
WHITE STONE, VIRGINIA
(ON THE RAPPAHANNOCK RIVER)
Dine and Sleep at the Water's Edge

View from the Rappahannock River showing White Stone Beach, Virginia. Circa 1950s; $10

The pier at White Stone Beach, Taft, Virginia. The handwritten message on the backside reads: "Jack and I are down here fishing but the fish aren't biting." Circa 1940s; $5

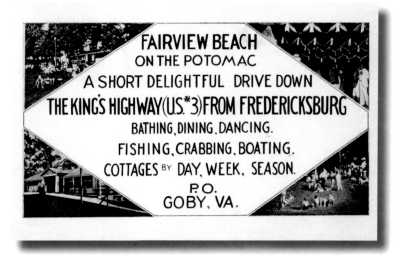

Fairview Beach is located on the Potomac River near Goby, Virginia. There was a wide sandy beach and lots of shaded picnic tables on the grounds. Postmarked 1942; $15

The snack bar at Fairview Beach, Virginia. Signs in the windows advertise souvenirs, sandwiches, and groceries. Postmarked 1956; $15

The beach and pavilion at Fairview Beach, Virginia. Circa 1930s; $8

Two different views of Fairview Beach, Virginia as seen from an airplane. One view shows the motorboat arriving and the other shows it leaving. Circa 1950s; $5

Fairview Beach, Virginia. The handwritten message on the backside reads: "You would like this place. The house on the water is in Maryland and has all kinds of slot machines. 100 degrees today." Circa 1950s; $5

The Pine Beach pavilion at Pine Beach, Virginia. Pine Beach was located on land that became a part of the U.S. Naval Operating Base. Circa 1907-12; $12

Uncle Billie's Snack Bar at North Beach, Maryland. Circa 1940s; $8

Uncle Billie's Amusement Center at North Beach, Maryland. Circa 1940s; $8

The bathing beach on the Chesapeake Bay at North Beach, Maryland. Circa 1930s; $7

Enjoying the beach at North Beach, Maryland. Circa 1930s; $7

Chapel Point was a popular bathing beach on the Port Tobacco River in Charles County, Maryland. The message on the backside reads: "Having a grand time here. The 'x' shows where we tied up, the 'o' shows where the children swim." Postmarked Aug. 1944; $8

Red Point Beach was located on the North East River in Cecil County, Maryland. The handwritten message on the backside reads: "We are staying in the 3rd cottage you see in this picture. It sure is a nice place." Postmarked Aug. 1951; $8

Breezy Point Beach is located directly on the Chesapeake Bay in Calvert County, Maryland. Circa 1930s; $8

View of the boardwalk at White Crystal Beach. Popular in the 1930s and 1940s, White Crystal Beach is located on the Elk River in Cecil County, Maryland. Circa 1930s; $6

HERALD HARBOR PARK

Maryland's Finest Beach Resort

ALPINE BEACH, THE IDEAL BEACH FOR SWIMMING—PICNICS

Alpine Beach was located where the Patapsco River meets the Chesapeake Bay in Anne Arundel County, Maryland. Its parking lot swelled to capacity on most summer weekends in the 1940s. Postmarked 1948; $10

Cottages at Port Herman Beach, Cecil Co., Md.

Herald Harbor Park was located in a protective cove on the Severn River at Herald Harbor, Maryland. It was a very popular bathing beach in the 1930s and 1940s. Circa 1940s; $10

Cottages at Port Herman Beach. The beach is located on the Elk River in Cecil County, Maryland. Postmarked 1938; $15

43

Mago Vista Beach was located on the Magothy River in Anne Arundel County, Maryland. Circa 1940s; $15

A shady spot at Crystal Beach Manor. The beach was located on the Elk River, near Earleville, Maryland.

Holloway Beach is located on the North East River near Charlestown in Cecil County, Maryland. The handwritten message on the backside reads: "Nicest beach, water clear, you can see the bottom." Circa 1940s; $15

44

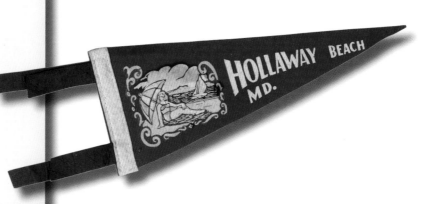

Bath House at Holloway Beach, Charlestown, Maryland. Circa 1940s; $25

A busy day at Holloway Beach, Charlestown, Maryland. Circa 1940s; $15

Happy bathers at Holloway Beach. Postmarked 1947; $15

Posing for the camera at Holloway Beach. Postmarked 1939; $15

Plenty of free parking at Holloway Beach, Maryland. Circa 1930s; $15

Enjoying a sail at Holloway Beach, Maryland. Postmarked 1938; $15

Riverview Park was an amusement park located on the Patapsco River a short distance from Baltimore. First known as Point Breeze, the park was nicknamed: "The Coney Island of the South." Circa 1907-12; $8

An elaborate carousel graced the grounds at Riverview Park. Circa 1907-12; $30

CAROUSEL. River View Park. Baltimore, Md.

MINIATURE RAILWAY. River View Park. Baltimore, Md.

THE CASINO
Riverview Park.

The miniature railroad at Riverview Park, Baltimore, Maryland. Postmarked 1909; $20

No. 156.

Baltimore, Md.

The casino and ferris wheel at Riverview Park near Baltimore, Maryland. Circa 1904-07; $25

When school was over, the time came to go to summer camp. There were quite a number of summer camps located on the Chesapeake Bay and along its rivers. In addition to an abundance of fresh air, sunshine, new friends, and campfires, the camps offered a variety of water sports. By the end of camp, one was certain to be a better swimmer, boater, and canoeist. Whether at camp for a week, a month, or for the entire summer, the camper brought back many lasting memories.

I remember going to summer camp when I was twelve. It was the Camp Conoy (now gone) in Calvert County, Maryland. When not taking part in some structured event, I spent my time walking the shoreline of the Chesapeake Bay and looking for fossilized sharks' teeth. By the end of camp, I had a big handful of the teeth in various sizes and shapes. Around the campfire, at night, the camp counselors told ghost stories, and one particular local tale about a big monster that lived in the woods nearby. Thinking about it now, that latter story was surely told with the intention of keeping us kids in our cabins after lights out. It was all a lot of fun, but by the end of summer camp, I must say, I had a greater appreciation for my mother's home cooking, and of having a bedroom all to myself.

VIEW SHOWING CAMP FACILITIES AND BAY
*Greetings from Camp Chesapeake*
OWNED AND OPERATED BY COATESVILLE Y. M. C. A.

Camp Chesapeake was located on the Elk River, near North East, Maryland. The handwritten message on the backside reads: "I am at Camp Chesapeake and am having a fun time. I have made many new friends. I did go swimming today. It is really fun. Love, Mary." Circa 1950s; $7

Camp Conoy was a Y.M.C.A. camp on the South River, near Edgewater, Maryland. *Note: This camp had the same name as the one near Lusby, Maryland.* Circa 1930; $10

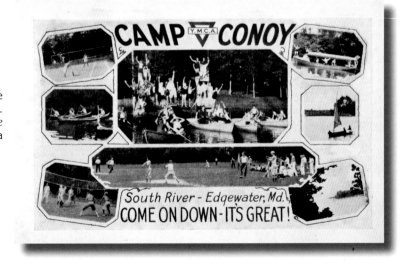

48

THE HOME OF GOOD EATS—CAMP CONOY

BOY'S PARADISE AT CAMP COLUMBUS, LEONARDTOWN, MARYLAND.

Camp Conoy was a camp for boys on the Chesapeake Bay near Lusby, Maryland. The dining hall was a popular place after spending the day looking for fossils along the Bay's shoreline. *Note: This camp had the same name as the one on the South River.* Circa 1930s; $15

Camp Columbus was a summer camp for boys near Leonardtown, Maryland. Circa 1920s; $8

"THE OLD SWIMMING HOLE" — CAMP LETTS, MD.

Camp Letts is a Y.M.C.A. summer camp for boys and girls on the Rhode River, near Mayo, Maryland. Swimming, sailing and fishing are amongst the activities that the camp offers. Circa 1930; $8

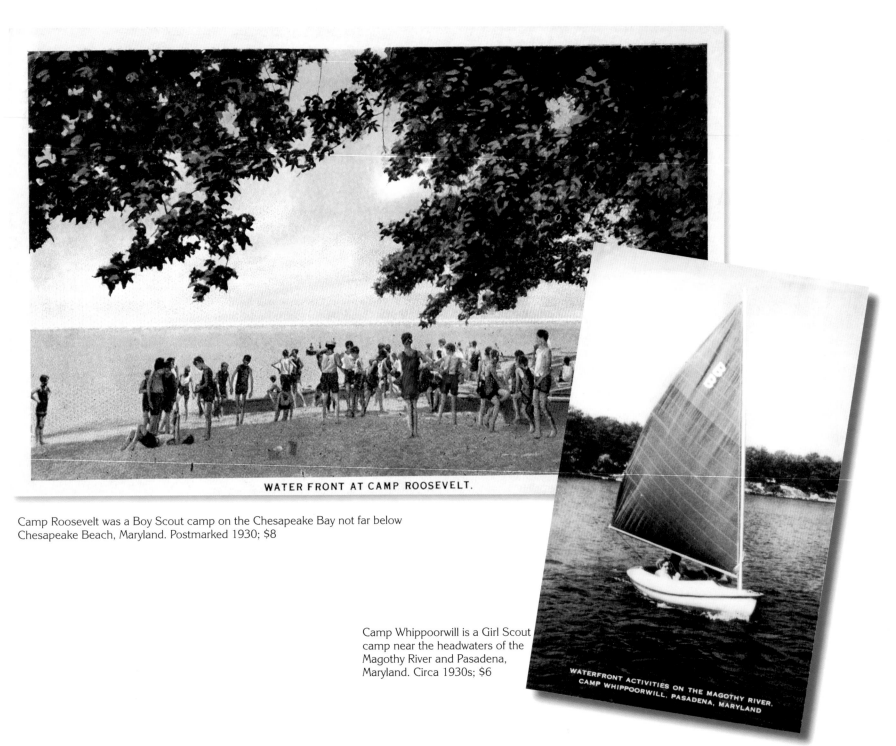

WATER FRONT AT CAMP ROOSEVELT.

Camp Roosevelt was a Boy Scout camp on the Chesapeake Bay not far below
Chesapeake Beach, Maryland. Postmarked 1930; $8

Camp Whippoorwill is a Girl Scout camp near the headwaters of the Magothy River and Pasadena, Maryland. Circa 1930s; $6

WATERFRONT ACTIVITIES ON THE MAGOTHY RIVER, CAMP WHIPPOORWILL, PASADENA, MARYLAND

Camp Pawatinika was a Y.W.C.A. summer camp located below Annapolis, Maryland on the South River. Postmarked 1936; $10

The Boy Scout camp at Oakwood Park Inn at St. Michaels, Maryland. Circa 1910-15; $30

Camp Wawanaissa was a summer camp for Campfire Girls. The camp was located on the Severn River in Anne Arundel County. Circa 1920s; $15

# Chapter 3
## BEFORE THE BRIDGES – FERRYBOATS

Before bridges linked opposite shores of the Chesapeake Bay with ribbons of cold steel and concrete, there were ferry boats. In Maryland, the Chesapeake Bay Ferry System operated a ferry service between Sandy Point and Matapeake. With the opening of the Chesapeake Bay Bridge in 1952, the ferry service was no longer needed and was terminated. Several ferries also operated in Virginia's Hampton Roads area. The Willoughby Spit-Old Point Ferry, the Norfolk-Portsmouth Ferry, and the Norfolk-Newport News Ferry became obsolete with the opening of the Hampton Roads Bridge-Tunnel in 1957. The opening of the Chesapeake Bay Bridge-Tunnel in 1964 brought an end to the Kiptopeke Beach–Little Creek Ferry service. Once the only way to cross, the ferry boats on the Chesapeake Bay were as important in their time as the Bay's bridges are today.

In 1919 the *Governor Emerson C. Harrington* was placed in service on the Claiborne - Annapolis Ferry route. Her foredeck was cut back to accommodate the carrying of autos. Postmarked 1928; $40

The *Governor Emerson C. Harrington* at Claiborne, Maryland. Clearly labeled on her port side is: "Claiborne – Annapolis Ferry Inc." Circa 1919; $40

Between the years 1923 and 1927 the steamer *Majestic* operated as a ferryboat between Claiborne and Annapolis, Maryland. Circa 1923; $15

53

The *Governor Albert C. Ritchie*, a 194 foot, double ended ferry was placed in service in 1926 on the Claiborne – Annapolis Ferry route. Circa 1926; $6

The Claiborne – Annapolis Ferry Company placed the 215 foot *John M. Dennis* in service in 1929. Circa 1929; $25

This is a later view of the double ended ferry, *John M. Dennis*. Circa 1930s; $15

The Chesapeake City, Maryland bridge over the Chesapeake & Delaware Canal was destroyed in July 1942 after being accidentally rammed by a 540 foot ship. To relieve the traffic problem this caused, the 40 vehicle ferryboat *Gotham* was placed in service at Chesapeake City. She operated on a 24 hour, fare free schedule until the new high level, arch bridge was opened in 1949. Circa 1942; $15

"Captain John Smith" ferry plying between Historic Jamestown Island, Va. and Scotland Neck.

The *Captain John Smith* navigated a narrow portion of the James River between Scotland and Jamestown, Virginia . Circa 1940s; $6

The New York, Philadelphia & Norfolk Railroad (Pennsylvania Railroad) operated ferry service between Cape Charles and Norfolk, Virginia. The steamer *Pennsylvania* was placed on the 36 mile route in 1900. Postmarked 1911; $15

Ferry Boat landing an Willoughby Beach, near Norfolk, Va.

Steamer Pennsylvania, Cape Charles, Va.

The Old Point Ferry operated across Hampton Roads between Old Point Comfort and Willoughby Spit, Virginia. Circa 1908-14; $7

The *Virginia Lee* was built in 1928 for the Pennsylvania Railroad's ferry service between Cape Charles and Norfolk, Virginia. She remained in service until she was requisitioned by the War Shipping Administration at the start of WWII. Circa 1930s; $15

S. S. VIRGINIA LEE

STEAMER PENNSYLVANIA AND GOVERNMENT JETTY, CAPE CHARLES, VA.

S. S. ELISHA LEE—Pennsylvania Railroad

The steamer *Pennsylvania* is shown approaching the government dock at Cape Charles. The trip between Cape Charles and Norfolk, Virginia took approximately 2 hours and 50 minutes. Circa 1920s; $10

The Pennsylvania Railroad operated the *S.S. Elisha Lee* between Norfolk, Old Point Comfort, and Cape Charles, Virginia between 1944 and 1953. Circa 1940s; $15

The *Princess Anne* was built in 1936 for the Virginia Ferry Corporation. She operated between Cape Charles and Little Creek, Virginia. In 1950 the company's northern terminal was moved from Cape Charles to Kiptopeke Beach. The *Princess Anne* was lengthened 90 feet in 1954. Circa 1930s; $8

Circa 1940s; $10

The 300 foot *S.S. Pocahontas* was built in 1941 for the Virginia Ferry Corporation. She was lengthened 76 feet in 1954. With the opening of the Chesapeake Bay Bridge Tunnel in 1964, the *Pocahontas* was the last vessel to make the ferry crossing between Little Creek and Kiptopeke Beach, Virginia on April 15, 1964. Circa 1950s; $4

"CITY OF HAMPTON". OLD POINT — WILLOUGHBY FERRY

The double ended ferryboat *City of Hampton* was built in 1930. She carried passengers and vehicles across Hampton Roads between Old Point Comfort and Willoughby Spit, Virginia. Circa 1930; $8

FERRY LANDING AT PINE BEACH, NORFOLK, VA.

NORFOLK—NEWPORT NEWS FERRY—THE POPULAR ROUTE

The double ended ferryboat *Hampton Roads* was built in 1925 for the Chesapeake Ferry Company. She operated on the Norfolk – Newport News route across Hampton Roads. Circa 1925; $5

"MIDDLE GROUND LIGHT." SCENE OF ENGAGEMENT BETWEEN THE MERRIMAC AND MONITOR

NORFOLK—NEWPORT NEWS FERRY—THE POPULAR ROUTE

Another view of the ferryboat *Hampton Roads*. She is shown passing Middle Ground Light in Hampton Roads. Circa 1925; $5

DOCKING AT NORFOLK TERMINAL, SHOWING LARGE SPACE FOR AUTOS.

NORFOLK—NEWPORT NEWS DIRECT FERRY ROUTE.

The *Hampton Roads* is shown docking at her Norfolk, Virginia terminal. Circa 1925; $5

FERRY "HAMPTON ROADS." 65 AUTO CAPACITY

2521-30

NORFOLK—NEWPORT NEWS FERRY—THE POPULAR ROUTE

The ferryboat *Hampton Roads* could carry 65 automobiles. Circa 1925; $5

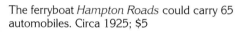

GLOUCESTER-YORKTOWN FERRY

"Ferryboat York," Gloucester and Yorktown Ferry.

The trip across the York River aboard the Gloucester-Yorktown Ferry took all but 8 minutes. The ferry operated 24 hours a day on the half hour. The handwritten message on the backside reads: This is the new ferryboat cross the York River. Holds 30 autos." Circa 1930s; $6

The summertime vacation – it's the opportunity to go someplace where less is more. The perfect spot for many city dwellers was a place in the country, where the trees gently sway to the cool breezes that blow off the Chesapeake Bay.

GREETINGS FROM THE SEASIDE.

Hotel Love Point at Love Point, Maryland. The hand-written message on the backside reads: "George and I are here for the weekend and it is a lovely place." Postmarked 1923; $15

The veranda of Hotel Love Point had plenty of chairs for guest to enjoy. Postmarked 1911; $30

The dining room at Hotel Love Point at Love Point, Maryland. Postmarked 1916; $35

The Hotel Fillmore at Love Point, Maryland. The handwritten message on the backside reads: "I took a ride down the Bay. It is a grand ride. We all enjoyed it very much, am waiting for supper at this hotel before taking the boat back to Baltimore." Postmarked 1915; $20

The Casino Hotel at Love Point, Maryland. In 1910 the hotel could accommodate 25 guests and the weekly rate was $8.00. Postmarked 1910; $15

The boardwalk, Love Point, Maryland. Circa 1907-12; $35

The Chesapeake House at Tilghman, Maryland. Circa 1920s; $15

Happy bathers with a sailboat at Tilghman, Maryland. Circa 1909-15; $35

The River Dale Hotel at Tilghman, Maryland. In 1910 the hotel could accommodate 60 guests and the weekly rate was $4.00. The handwritten message on the backside reads: "We arrived safe here at Tilghman and found everyone well, also plenty of water." Postmarked 1922; $20

Perry Cabin, St. Michaels, Maryland. The handwritten message on the backside reads: "We are spending the night in this lovely old town." Postmarked 1951; $8

The Willows at St. Michaels, Maryland. Postmarked 1910; $20

Bathing at the Oakwood Park Inn at St. Michaels, Maryland. Circa 1909-15; $20

Near St. Michaels, Maryland, Wades Point Inn with its panoramic views of the Chesapeake Bay and the Eastern Bay has been a popular escape from the city for nearly 100 years. Circa 1930s; $8

Enjoying a cool dip in the water at Maple Hall Farm in Claiborne, Maryland. Postmarked 1924; $20

White Hall at Royal Oak, Maryland. In 1910 the guest house could accommodate 50 guests and the weekly rate was $6.00. Circa 1910-15; $20

The Pasadena Inn at Royal Oak, Maryland. In 1910 the guest house could accommodate 100 guests and the weekly rate was $7.00. Postmarked 1923; $20

Bathing beauties at the Pasadena Inn in Royal Oak, Maryland. Circa 1930s; $10

A raft full of swimmers at Pasadena Inn in Royal Oak, Maryland. Postmarked 1943; $7

Boating, Bathing, Fishing and Crabbing at Sylvan Shores, Washington nearest and newest Salt Water Beach and Summer Home Colony. Furnished cottages for rent or for sale on easy terms. Carl W. Riddick, owner and developer, Riva, Md.

Boating, Bathing, Fishing, and Crabbing at Sylvan Shores on the South River near Riva, Maryland. Circa 1920s; $8

SWANN'S HOTEL AT PINEY POINT, MD.

Swan's Hotel at Piney Point, Maryland on the Potomac River. The handwritten message on the backside reads: "This is the hotel we stayed at. I caught two fish yesterday. Today the Potomac is foggy. Went fishing but didn't get a nibble. Morgantown Ferry across Potomac River 4:50 P.M., distance across 4 1/4 miles, charge $1.25, time 45 minutes."

"THERE'S ALWAYS A BREEZE AT POINT LOOKOUT HOTEL"

POINT LOOKOUT HOTEL, POINT LOOKOUT, MD.

The Point Lookout Hotel at Point Lookout, Maryland and the mouth of the Potomac River. Postmarked 1939; $8

ADAMS' HOTEL
ST. GEORGE'S ISLAND, ST. MARY'S COUNTY
MARYLAND

1913

The Adams Hotel and Pier at St. George Island on the Potomac River. Postmarked 1913; $15

Views at Blenhorn Farm, Wm. J. Youngman, Prop., Woolford, Md.

Views of the Blenhorn Farm at Woolford, Maryland. Vacationing in Dorchester County and enjoying the Little Choptank River. Circa 1909-12; $7

Vacationing at the Blenhorn Farm at Woolford, Maryland. Postmarked 1909; $7

Horn's Point overlooking the Choptank River at Cambridge, Maryland. Circa 1920s; $8

Plum Point Cottage at Plum Point. Plum Point sits on the Chesapeake Bay and is located in Calvert County, Maryland. Postmarked 1912; $15

The St. Mary's church, the lighthouse at Piney Point, and the Potomac River in southern Maryland. Circa 1904-07; $15

Hotel Bellefonte overlooked the Eastern Bay at Claiborne, Maryland. Circa 1920s; $20

Tourist home at Neavitt, Maryland. Neavitt sits out at the end of a long point in Talbot County. It is nearly surrounded by Harris Creek, Broad Creek, and the Choptank River.

The beach, bath house, and Evans Hotel at Waterview Beach, Maryland. Circa 1915-20; $8

The Great Oak Lodge on the Chesapeake Bay and Fairlee Creek, east of Chestertown, Maryland. Circa 1950s; $10

The Oakley Beach Hotel at Cambridge, Maryland. Circa 1920; $8

High View Guest House overlooking the Chesapeake Bay at Chesapeake Beach, Maryland took in guests for the entire summer season. Circa 1940s; $12

The Scotland Beach Hotel at Scotland Beach, Maryland. Scotland Beach is located on the Chesapeake Bay in southern Saint Mary's County. Circa 1930; $25

The Scotland Beach Hotel on the Chesapeake Bay at Scotland Beach, Maryland. The handwritten message on the backside reads: "Down here, 2 miles from Pt. Lookout, MD. Fine bathing and everything lovely." Postmarked 1930; $25

Mogart's Beach is located on the south shore of the James River, a short distance from Smithfield, Virginia. Circa 1930s; $8

The large Terminal Hotel at West Point, Virginia. West Point is located at the headwaters of the York River. The Chesapeake Steamship Company operated their steamers between Baltimore, Maryland and landings on the York River for years. Rail connection could be had at West Point for those going on to Richmond, Virginia and beyond. It was a 198 mile trip by water between Baltimore and West Point. Postmarked 1910; $10

It was a relaxed way of life at the Riverview Cottage overlooking the Rappahannock River at Sharps, Virginia. Circa 1930s; $10

SHELLFIELD-ON-THE-POTOMAC

WILKERSON, VA.

Wilkerson, Virginia, now known as Potomac Beach is located
a short distance up the Potomac River from Colonial Beach,
Virginia. Circa 1930s; $8

IRVINGTON BEACH HOTEL
On Carter Creek    Irvington, Va.
Boating — Bathing — Fishing

9605

The Irvington Beach Hotel on Carter's Creek in Irvington, Virginia
offered boating, bathing, and fishing. Postmarked 1939; $8

THE TIDES INN AND DOCK -- IRVINGTON, VIRGINIA    C41

The Tides Inn overlooks Carter's Creek at Irvington,
Virginia. Postmarked 1950; $8

Sea Breeze, Cape Henry, Va.

The Sea Breeze at
Cape Henry, Virginia.
Circa 1912; $10

HOTEL SAMORE, STINGRAY POINT, DELTAVILLE, VA.

Urbanna Beach Hotel, Urbanna, Va.

5728

Hotel Samore at Stingray Point on the Chesapeake
Bay, near Deltaville, Virginia. Circa 1940s; $8

The Urbanna Beach Hotel on the Rappahannock
River at Urbanna, Virginia offered relaxation far
removed from the city. Circa 1930s; $8

The Chesapeake Bay sits in the direct path of the Atlantic Flyway. Thus the Bay is the winter home to numerous species of waterfowl, including ducks, swans, and geese. The canvasback duck is a favorite of the hunter and a special delicacy at the dinner table. The ducks begin to find their way into the Chesapeake region in October with the majority showing up in mid November through early December. The favored location for the hunter in search of the canvasback has long been the western shore of the upper Bay, particularly the area known as the Susquehanna Flats at the headwaters of the Bay.

With over two hundred species of fish, the Chesapeake Bay has been called an "Angler's Paradise." The Chesapeake's principal game fish are channel bass, black drum, bluefish, rockfish, trout, hardhead, spot, and perch. Striped bass, or rockfish as they are generally called, are a particularly prized catch. The fish grow to a large size, put up a good fight at the end of the line, and are widely considered to be one of the best-tasting of the aquatic species to ever be dropped into a cook's skillet. Rockfish are found throughout the Bay. Spring and fall are the best times to fish for them.

DUCK SHOOTING AT HAVRE-DE-GRACE, MD.

Duck hunting from a sink box on the Susquehanna Flats at Havre de Grace, Maryland. Circa 1916-25; $10

A hunter in a sink box surrounded by decoys at Havre de Grace, Maryland. Postmarked 1907; $15

Duck Shooting from sink box, Havre de Grace, Maryland.

Shooting ducks from a sink box on the Susquehanna Flats at Havre de Grace, Maryland. Postmarked 1909; $10

RAIL BIRD SHOOTING, HAVRE DE GRACE, MD.
4219

Hunting from a small boat in the marshes, near Havre de Grace. Circa 1904-07; $12

A DUCK HUNTER'S DREAM AT CRISFIELD, MD.

The result of a day spent duck hunting on Maryland's lower Eastern Shore, near Crisfield, Maryland. Circa 1916-25; $10

BOWEN'S FISHING FLEET
One of the Largest and best equipped on the Bay
Fishing Parties Day and Night
Bowen's Inn, Solomons. Md.     Phone: Solomons 416

Charter fishing boats at Solomons, Maryland. Circa 1930s-40s; $10

FISHING IS GOOD AT OCEAN VIEW, NEAR NORFOLK, VA.—17

A nice string of fish caught at Ocean View, Virginia. Circa 1916-20; $8

The big one that didn't get away at Piney Point, Maryland. Postmarked 1950; $8

SWANN'S HOTEL    PINEY POINT, MARYLAND

FISHING PARTY ON CHOPTANK RIVER, MARYLAND
PUB. BY M. WARREN HOOPER, STATIONER

The result of fishing on the Choptank River. Circa 1907-12; $15

A CATCH -- THE TIDES INN -- IRVINGTON, VIRGINIA  C29

A good day's catch at Irvington, Virginia. Circa 1950s; $8

WINDY T FISHING PARTY BOAT—ROD & REEL DOCK—CHESAPEAKE BEACH, MD.

The charter fishing boat *Windy T* left daily from the Rod and Reel Dock at Chesapeake Beach, Maryland. Postmarked 1956; $7

Proud fishermen with their catch at the Oakwood Inn, St. Michaels, Maryland. Circa 1930s; $8

The Chesapeake House at Tilghman, Maryland. The handwritten message on the backside reads: "This is an ideal spot for fishing. We stayed at this house, went fishing on this boat, on Chesapeake Bay and caught sixty (60) fish. This is the truth." Circa 1938-43; $10

FIRST TURN TO LEFT, SECOND HOUSE AFTER LEAVING TILGHMAN BRIDGE

PHONE 4251

"POPLAR GROVE"
MODERN CONVENIENCES

CAPT. LUTHER GARVIN
FISHING PARTIES ACCOMMODATED
TILGHMAN, MARYLAND
LARGE ROOMY BOATS — EXPERT GUIDES

Charter fishing boat at Tilghman, Maryland. Circa 1930s-40s; $10

The charter fishing boat *Sylvia J* at Tilghman, Maryland. Circa 1930s-40s; $10

Home with a catch of fish at Fairbank, Maryland. Circa 1920s; $12

Catching the Blues, at Solomons, Maryland. Circa 1920s; $8

A ride on an excursion boat offered a mini escape, a one day vacation, an outing to a place where relaxation, sun, fun, good food, and thrills were all merged together. The day trip would be planned weeks in advance. On the big day, picnic baskets would be stuffed with fried chicken and deviled eggs, kids would be dressed in their best, and past trips would be recounted one last time. Everyone rode the excursion boats at least once a season and onboard would be found new lovers, newlyweds, and new babies. The excursion boat companies catered to families small, large, and extended. Discounts would be given to church groups, clubs, and employee groups that booked in advance. Depending on the day, there would be several hundred or several thousand exuberant passengers full of smiles and laughter. After a long day spent at the beach, the mood on the way back would be much more somber, broken only by a child's misplaced laughter or the cries of a baby. It was a time to lean against the boat's rail, watch the last rays of the sun bounce off its wake, reflect on the happy time, and make a vow to do it all again – soon.

The 232 foot steamer *Louise* was built in 1864. Her original owner, the Morgan Line placed her in service on the Gulf of Mexico, operating between New Orleans, Louisiana and Mobile, Alabama. She was named after the daughter of the Morgan Line's owner. The Baltimore, Chesapeake and Richmond Steamboat Company purchased the Louise in 1874. In 1885 the Tolchester Steamboat Company acquired her. She carried upwards of 2,500 excursionists at any one time on her trips between Baltimore and Tolchester Beach, Maryland. *Louise* was sold to a New York concern in 1926. Circa 1907-12; $7

STEAMER LOUISE, MOONLIGHT ON THE CHESAPEAKE.

Two views showing the steamer *Louise* draped in
moonlight on the Chesapeake Bay. Circa 1916-20; $8

Steamer *Louise*, by moonlight on the way to Tolchester Beach, Md.

Steamer "Susquehanna,"
near Havre De Grace, Md.

SUSQUEHANNA

The 158 foot *Susquehanna* was built in 1898 for the Tolchester Steamboat Company. She operated between Baltimore and landings on the upper Chesapeake. She also served as an excursion
boat to Betterton and Tolchester Beach, Maryland. The *Susquehanna* was sold to a Louisiana
concern in 1923. In 1941 she was returned to Chesapeake waters, renamed *Francis Scott Key*
and under Tolchester Lines, Inc., ran excursions from Baltimore to Tolchester Beach from 1941
to 1943. Circa 1908-12; $15

The 165 foot *Cambridge* was built in 1890 for the Choptank Steamboat Company. In 1894 she came under the control of the Baltimore, Chesapeake and Atlantic Railway Company. She was placed on the company's Baltimore to Claiborne route. In 1924 her Eastern Shore terminus was switched from Claiborne to Love Point, Maryland. Postmarked 1924; $30

This early 1900s view shows the steamer *Cambridge* on the Patapsco River, near Baltimore. At the time she was being operated by the Baltimore, Chesapeake and Atlantic Railway Company on their Baltimore to Claiborne route. At Claiborne in Talbot County, passengers had the option of continuing as far as Ocean City, Maryland via the company's railway division. Circa 1904-07; $15

The steamer *Annapolis* was built in 1892 as the 151 foot steamer *Sassafras* for the Sassafras River Steamboat Company. In 1902 she came under the control of the Tolchester Steamboat Company which had her lengthened 25 feet and renamed her *Annapolis*. Postmarked 1907; $15

Steamer Dreamland, Baltimore, Md.

From 1909 to 1925 the 273 foot *Dreamland* operated as an excursion boat between Baltimore and Chesapeake Beach, Maryland. Circa 1909; $12

The 136 foot steamer *Kitty Knight* was built in 1860 as the *Van Corlaer the Trumpeter*. In 1913 the *Kitty Knight* came under the control of the Rock Creek Steamboat Company. She operated between Baltimore and the various landings on Rock Creek until 1924. Circa 1913-16; $12

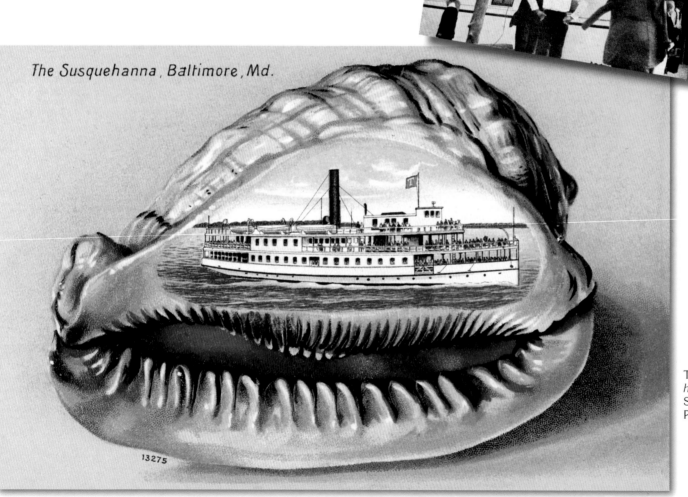

The Susquehanna, Baltimore, Md.

13275

The 158 foot steamer *Susquehanna* flying the Tolchester Steamboat Company flag. Postmarked 1908. $15

The Maryland, Delaware and Virginia Railway Company's steamer *Love Point* began operating between Baltimore and Love Point Maryland in 1906. She left the Pier 7, Light Street wharf twice daily in the summer months. Circa 1908; $30

In the early 1900s, a trip from Baltimore to the white sands and crescent waves at Rehoboth Beach, Delaware was not the one tank of gas, routine trip that it is today. The shortest, quickest, and about the only way was via the steamer and then the train of the Maryland, Delaware and Virginia Railway Company. One boarded the steamer in the morning, for the 2 hour, 27 mile trip down and across the Bay to Love Point, Maryland. At Love Point connection was made with a waiting train. The train carried its occupants through the Eastern Shore countryside, past the towns of Queenstown, Denton, Greenwood, and Lewis. Then as stomachs started to stir for dinner, the train arrived at Rehoboth Beach, Delaware. Circa 1908; $30

This promotional postcard of the Baltimore, Chesapeake and Atlantic Railway Company invites the excursionist to take a trip on their steamer from Baltimore to Claiborne, Maryland. Circa 1908; $30

The 180 foot *Maryland* was built in 1902 for the Baltimore, Chesapeake and Atlantic Railway Company. The Maryland operated on the company's Pocomoke River route. Circa 1908; $30

Part of the fun was in the getting there, and so it was with the trip to Ocean City, Maryland in the early 1900s. First one boarded the Baltimore, Chesapeake and Atlantic Railway Company's steamer at Pier 4 Light Street in Baltimore. Then a 3 hour, 44 mile boat ride down the Bay found one at Claiborne in Talbot County on Maryland's Eastern Shore. From Claiborne, the Baltimore, Chesapeake and Atlantic's, Ocean City Express train ran direct, without any stops to the wind swept ocean resort. Circa 1908; $30

The steamer *Love Point*, formerly *Emma A. Ford*, was placed on the Maryland, Delaware and Virginia Railway's, Baltimore to Love Point, Maryland route in 1906. In 1909 she burned beyond repair at Love Point. Circa 1907; $20

ON BOARD MARYLAND, DELAWARE AND VIRGINIA RAILWAY'S STEAMER LOVE POINT
"THE LOVE POINT TRIP"

Steamer Dreamland at Love Point, Md.

DREAMLAND.

The 273 foot steamer *Dreamland* was built in 1878 as the *Republic*. She was brought to the Chesapeake Bay from New York in 1908 and placed in service between Baltimore and Love Point, Maryland. In 1909 she began carrying excursionists to Chesapeake Beach, Maryland. Circa 1908; $15

STEAMER "EXPRESS", BALTIMORE'S LARGEST EXCURSION STEAMER.

STEAMER "DIXIE". Chesapeake Bay Trip, To Seaside Park, Md.

The Wilson Line's four-decker *S.S. Dixie* went from Baltimore to Seaside Park, Maryland from 1936 until 1942. Circa 1930s; $15

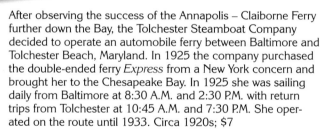

After observing the success of the Annapolis – Claiborne Ferry further down the Bay, the Tolchester Steamboat Company decided to operate an automobile ferry between Baltimore and Tolchester Beach, Maryland. In 1925 the company purchased the double-ended ferry *Express* from a New York concern and brought her to the Chesapeake Bay. In 1925 she was sailing daily from Baltimore at 8:30 A.M. and 2:30 P.M. with return trips from Tolchester at 10:45 A.M. and 7:30 P.M. She operated on the route until 1933. Circa 1920s; $7

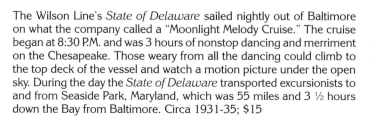

STEAMER "STATE OF DELAWARE" OF THE WILSON LINE FLEET

The Wilson Line's *State of Delaware* sailed nightly out of Baltimore on what the company called a "Moonlight Melody Cruise." The cruise began at 8:30 P.M. and was 3 hours of nonstop dancing and merriment on the Chesapeake. Those weary from all the dancing could climb to the top deck of the vessel and watch a motion picture under the open sky. During the day the *State of Delaware* transported excursionists to and from Seaside Park, Maryland, which was 55 miles and 3 ½ hours down the Bay from Baltimore. Circa 1931-35; $15

The steamer *St. Johns* carried thousands on the Potomac River between Washington, D.C. and Colonial Beach, Virginia between the years 1906 and 1927. The handwritten message on the backside reads: "On our Sunday school picnic we went down the Potomac River." Postmarked 1911; $30

The *Tolchester* carried excursionists from Baltimore to Tolchester Beach, Maryland from 1949 until the end of the 1955 season. Circa 1950s; $10

S. S. TOLCHESTER, FROM BALTIMORE TO TOLCHESTER BEACH, MARYLAND, ON CHESAPEAKE BAY

The 315 foot steamer *S.S. Potomac* was built as the *Albany* for the Hudson River Day Line in 1880. Between 1934 and 1948 she operated as an excursion boat between Washington, D.C. and Colonial Beach, Virginia. Circa 1940s; $10

S. S. "POTOMAC" — WASHINGTON'S LARGEST AND FASTEST EXCURSION STEAMER    9A-H378

The Wilson Line's *Bay Belle* ushered excursionists from Baltimore to Tolchester Beach and Betterton, Maryland in the late 1950s. Circa 1950s; $7

Marshall Hall was an amusement park located a short distance down the Potomac River from Washington, D.C., near Fort Washington, Maryland. The steamer *Charles Macalester*, shown here in 1907, could carry 1700 excursionist. The boat made two trips daily, at 10 A.M. and 2:30 P.M., to the park from her dock at the foot of Seventh Street. Circa 1907; $30

Steamer *Charles Macalester* and the dock at Fort Washington, Maryland. Notice the lighthouse beyond the trees. Circa 1907-15; $30

The Wilson Line's boat, *S.S. Mount Vernon,* is shown here on the Potomac River. She had a capacity of 2400 and sailed several times daily from pier four in Washington, D.C.. She stopped at George Washington's home in Mount Vernon, Virginia and then crossed the river to Marshall Hall Amusement Park located close the Fort Washington, Maryland. Circa 1950s; $4

Lighthouses serve two important purposes: they mark hazards to navigation, and their structures and lights are recognizable markers from which a navigational bearing can be taken. Three different types of lighthouses have been built on the Chesapeake Bay: the tower, the screwpile, and the caisson. The tower is basically just that, a tall tower painted or otherwise marked in a way to make it distinguishable from other lighthouses. Its tall tower enables the mariner to see it and its light from a great distance. Screwpile construction was popular on sandy or muddy bottoms. The screwpile style lighthouse consists of a structure resting on six or eight metal poles. The poles were literally screwed into the bottom by way of a metal screw-type flange which was attached to the lower part of each pole. Caisson-style lighthouses were made by lowering a large iron cylinder to the bottom. Normally, the water was then pumped out and the cylinder was lowered further to sit on a stable bottom, such as bedrock. The cylinder would then be filled with rocks or concrete and a structure containing the light erected on top of the cylinder.

Many of the Chesapeake Bay's lighthouses have been lost forever. A number have lost their superstructures and have modern, automated lights attached to their foundations. A couple of lighthouses have been moved from their original locations, restored, and are now museum pieces. A handful of lighthouses remain intact, still doing their intended job, guiding the mariner at sea.

Concord Point Lighthouse stands at the mouth of the Susquehanna River in Havre de Grace, Maryland. The 39 foot stone tower was erected in 1807. Circa 1907-12; $10

POINT CONCORD LIGHT HOUSE, HAVRE DE GRACE, MD.

Concord Point Lighthouse. Postmarked 1905; $10

Turkey Point Lighthouse is a 35 foot stone tower built in 1833. The lighthouse sits on a high bluff at the mouth of the Elk River. Circa 1930; $15

The Craighill Channel Upper Range (Front Light), also known as the North Point Light, is located on the Patapsco River in front of Fort Howard. The octagonal brick tower was erected in 1886. Circa 1904-07; $15

Construction of the Sevenfoot Knoll Lighthouse began in 1854. The Lighthouse sat out in the Bay at the mouth of the Patapsco River. In 1988 the lighthouse was moved and put on display at Baltimore's Inner Harbor. Circa 1904-07; $15

Craighill Channel Front Beacon (MAN OF WAR SHOAL LIGHT HOUSE) is located out into the bay, almost directly in front of pier, S. E. of Bay Shore Park. It has two fixed white lights, the upper visible 11½ miles, the lower in axes of channel only. The upper light can be seen from the park at night.

Baltimore, Md, Lazzerreto Light House

The Lazaretto Point Lighthouse was built in 1831 on a point of land, directly opposite of Fort McHenry and at the entrance to Baltimore's Northwest Harbor. The lighthouse was decommissioned in 1926 and torn down the same year. A replica of the lighthouse now stands at the site of the original lighthouse. Circa 1907-12; $6

The Craighill Channel Front Beacon was built in 1873. It sits out in the Chesapeake off North Point, near the mouth of the Patapsco River. The lighthouse is also known as the Front Lower Range Light and the Man of War Shoal Light. Circa 1904-07; $15

The Drum Point Lighthouse, built 1883, was located near the mouth of the Patuxent River. It has been moved and now is on display at the Calvert Marine Museum in Solomons, Maryland. Postmarked 1908; $25

DRUM POINT LIGHT HOUSE,

Patuxent River, near Solomon's, Md

Craighill Channel Rear Beacon(MILLERS ISLAND LIGHT HOUSE)is located at the head of the Bay, N. E. of Bay Shore Park. It has a fixed white light, visible 16 miles in axes of the channel only, which can be seen at night from the end of pier.

The Craighill Channel Rear Beacon was constructed in 1873. It is located on the Chesapeake Bay near North Point State Park in Baltimore County, Maryland. The lighthouse is also known as the Rear Lower Range Light and the Millers Island Light. Circa 1904-07; $15

The Point Lookout Lighthouse, built in 1830. The two story keeper's house and the lighthouse tower were built as one unit. The lighthouse is located at Point Lookout on the North Shore of the Potomac River. Circa 1920s; $30

OLD LIGHTHOUSE (Built 1836) AND BELL TOWER, PINEY POINT, MD.

The Piney Point Lighthouse was built in 1836. It is located on the Potomac River at Piney Point, Maryland. Circa 1930s; $25

Gough Bar Light House

The Great Wicomico Lighthouse (Gough Bar) was built in 1889. It was located at the mouth of the Great Wicomico River in Virginia. The lighthouse was fully automated in 1955. The wooden lighthouse structure was torn down in 1967 and an automated beacon was mounted on top of its screwpile foundation. Circa 1920s; $25

Light House, Fortress Monroe, Va.

The Old Point Comfort Lighthouse was constructed in 1802. It is located at Fort Monroe, Virginia. Circa 1908-12; $10

The Back River Lighthouse stood near the southern entrance to Virginia's Back River. The lighthouse was built in 1829. It was decommissioned in 1936. The lighthouse was destroyed in a 1956 hurricane. Circa 1920; $6

LIGHTHOUSE ON NEW POINT BEACH, MATHEWS COUNTY, VA.

THE BACK RIVER LIGHTHOUSE NEAR FORTRESS MONROE, VA.

Copyrighted by

The New Point Comfort Lighthouse was constructed in 1804. The white stone tower sits near the entrance to Mobjack Bay. Circa 1940s; $8

Thimble Shoal Lighthouse was constructed in the 1880s. The structure was destroyed by fire in 1909. It was replaced by a caisson style lighthouse in 1914. Circa 1908; $10

Thimble Shoal Light, Va.

CAPE CHARLES LIGHT, NEAR CAPE CHARLES, VA.

4004-29

The Windmill Point Lighthouse was constructed in 1869. It sat in 12 feet of water on the northerly side of the mouth of the Rappahannock River. The lighthouse was dismantled in 1965. Circa 1907-12; $10

The Cape Charles Lighthouse was constructed in 1895. The height of the light is 180 feet above mean high water and the light can be seen for 24 miles. Circa 1920s; $15

The lighthouse to the right is the first Cape Henry Lighthouse. Constructed in 1791, it is the oldest lighthouse on the Chesapeake Bay. The New Cape Henry Lighthouse, shown to the left, was constructed in 1881. Circa 1920s; $15

Circa 1940s; $7

Circa 1920s; $8

The lights from three Chesapeake Bay light-houses pierce the night's darkness.

Circa 1920s; $7

Transportation and commerce in the mid-Atlantic region was, at one time, dependent on the steamboats that traversed the many rivers of the Chesapeake Bay. If we think of the Chesapeake Bay in modern terms, its main channel was a super highway, its rivers were roads, and its creeks were country lanes. Riverboats keeping regular or semi-regular schedules were the trucks and taxies of the day, transporting both freight and passengers. The riverboats operated year-round and in all types of weather. Freight included farm produce, seafood, timber, tobacco, and all sorts of animals. For those living in the country, the riverboats brought such items as a new wood stove, farm machinery and even an occasional city dress for a country gal. The arrival of the riverboat at the local landing was a widely anticipated event. On the dock, the waiting passengers would give their city clothes one last look over as they shifted their weight from one leg to the other. Farmers stood by the horses in front of their wagons, or checked the water in the Model T's radiator while casually talking to one another and puffing on their pipes. Then suddenly someone would spot the boat down river and shout out "there she is." The riverboat's whistle would loudly sing out on its approach and waves stirred. On the boat, orders were given, lines were handed off, and the freight door opened. A flurry of activity ensued with the loading and offloading of freight and passengers. Kids laughed, babies just awakened by the noise would cry. Occasionally, an escaped chicken or pig added to the drama of the big event.

The *Talbot* and her sister ship the *Dorchester* were built in 1912 for the Baltimore, Chesapeake & Atlantic Railway Co. and placed on the company's Choptank River route The *Talbot* was 192 feet long. In 1929, under the Baltimore and Virginia Steamboat Company, the *Talbot* was placed in service on the Potomac River. In 1936 she was sold and went to New York state where she was renamed *City of New York*. Circa 1912; $15

Steamer "Talbot," Baltimore, Chesapeake and Atlantic Ry. Co., in service between Baltimore and Choptank River.

Steamer "Dorchester," Baltimore, Chesapeake & Atlantic Ry. Co., in service between Baltimore and Choptank River.

The *Dorchester* and her sister ship the *Talbot* were built in 1912 for the Baltimore, Chesapeake & Atlantic Railway Co. and placed on the company's Choptank River route. The ship was 192 feet long. In 1917 The *Dorchester* was withdrawn from the Choptank River route. In 1920 she was placed on the Potomac River route. She was sold to the Baltimore and Virginia Steamboat Company in 1928. In 1936 she was sold, renamed the *Robert E. Lee*, and operated out of Washington D.C. Circa 1912; $15

The *Three Rivers* was built in 1910 for the Maryland, Delaware and Virginia Railway and placed on the company's Potomac River Route. In 1923 she came under the control of the Baltimore and Virginia Steamboat Company. The *Three Rivers* burned on July 5, 1924 off of Cove Point while returning to Baltimore from Crisfield, Maryland. Circa 1910-12; $15

Steamer "Three Rivers," Maryland, Delaware and Virginia Railway Company, plying between Baltimore, Md., and Washington, D. C

THREE RIVERS

The steamer *Joppa* is shown docked at the wharf at Cambridge, Maryland. Postmarked 1910; $15

*Emma Giles* picking up passengers at the wharf in Annapolis, Maryland. Circa 1916-1925; $15

The *Virginia* was built in 1903 for the Baltimore, Chesapeake and Atlantic Railway Co. She was placed in service on the company's Wicomico River route. Here she is shown at the wharf in Salisbury, Maryland. Circa 1916-20; $10

Shady Side Steamer, Shady Side, Md.

The steamer *Shady Side* operated on the West River near Shady Side, Maryland. Circa 1908 – 1912; $15

B. C. & A. Pier, Sharp'own, Md.

One of the steamers of the Baltimore, Chesapeake and Atlantic Railway Co. is shown at the wharf in Sharptown, Maryland on the Nanticoke River. Postmarked 1907; $15

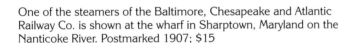

Steamer Emma Giles.

The 178 foot *Emma Giles* was built in 1887 for the Tolchester Steamboat Company. During the week she navigated between Baltimore and landings on the Miles, Little Choptank, West, South, and Rhode Rivers. On the weekends or when needed she helped to ferry excursionist between Baltimore and company's popular resort at Tolchester Beach, Maryland. In her later years she ran to landings on the Sassafras and Susquehanna Rivers. Circa 1907-12; $15

SCENE AT FEDERALSBURG, MD.

Steamer *Granite City* at Federalsburg, Maryland. Postmarked 1906; $15

*Emma A. Ford* was built in 1884 for the Chester River Steamboat Company. She operated between Baltimore and landings on the Chester River. In 1905 she was acquired by the Maryland, Delaware and Virginia Railway Company. In 1906 she was renamed *Love Point* and placed on the Baltimore to Love Point, Maryland route. Circa 1907-09; $15

The steamer *Joppa* was built in 1885 for the Maryland Steamboat Company. In 1894 her ownership was transferred to the newly formed Baltimore, Chesapeake & Atlantic Railway Company. *Joppa* operated between Baltimore and the landings on the Choptank River until 1929. Circa 1907-10; $35

Waiting for the steamboat to arrive at the Town Point wharf on the Elk River in Cecil county, Maryland. Postmarked 1912; $15

The 108 foot *West River* was built in 1907. Here she is shown at Hartge's Wharf on the West River, near Galesville, Maryland. Circa 1907; $20

The Baltimore, Chesapeake and Atlantic Railway Company steamer *Joppa* is shown at the wharf in Denton, Maryland. Circa 1909-12; $25

The steamer *West River* at the wharf in Annapolis, Maryland. Circa 1907-12; $20

Arrival at Havre de Grace, Md.

Steamer Annapolis

Steamer *Annapolis* underway on the upper waters of the Chesapeake Bay. Postmarked 1909; $20

The steamer *Northumberland* of the Maryland, Delaware and Virginia Railway Company is shown at the Leonardtown, Maryland wharf on Breton Bay. Circa 1907; $20

Steamer Pocomoke leaving Wharf, Onancock, Va.

The 170 foot steamer *Pocomoke* was built in 1891 for the Eastern Shore Steamboat Company. In 1905 she came under the control of the Baltimore, Chesapeake and Atlantic Railway Company. She operated on the Pocomoke and Nanticoke Rivers as well as landings on Virginia's Eastern Shore. Here we see her leaving the wharf at Onancock, Virginia. Circa 1907-12; $15

Wharf, Merry Point, Va.

STR. ANNE ARUNDEL-CAPT. W. C. GEOGHEGAN-LANDING AT BUSHWOOD WHARF.

PUBLISHED BY
W. W. BLAKISTONE,
BLAKISTONE, MD.

Busy wharf scene at Merry Point, Virginia. Circa 1909-15; $15

The steamer *Anne Arundel* landing at Bushwood Wharf on the Wicomico River in St. Mary's County, Maryland. The 174 foot vessel was built in 1904 for the Weems Line. Circa 1904; $20

STEAMER B. S. FORD, APPROACHING PIER, ROCK HALL, MD.

The *B.S. Ford* was built in 1877 for the Chester River Steamboat Company. She was acquired by the Maryland, Delaware and Virginia Railway in 1905 but remained on the Baltimore to Chester River route. Here we see her at the wharf at Rock Hall, Maryland. Postmarked 1915; $10

STEAMER B. S. FORD LEAVING WHARF, CHESTERTOWN, MD.

Steamer *B.S. Ford* leaving the wharf at Chestertown, Maryland. Postmarked 1924; $10

Coan Wharf, Northumberland County, Virginia.

A. D. DART, PUBLISHER

Steamer at Coan Wharf, Virginia on the Coan River. Postmarked 1910; $15

The steamer *Middlesex* was built in 1902 for the Weems Steamboat Company and placed on their Baltimore and Rappahannock River route. In 1905 her ownership was transferred to the Maryland, Delaware & Virginia Railway Co. The *Middlesex* is shown here leaving the dock at Irvington, Virginia. Postmarked 1919; $15

Steamer Middlesex leaving the dock at Irving'on, Va.

Claremont, Va. Wharf, Steamer Pocahontas.

Claremont is located up the James River in Surry County, Virginia. Here the Old Dominion Line steamer *Pocahontas* is shown at the Claremont wharf. Postmarked 1912; $15

Steamer at the wharf, Kinsale, Virginia on the Yeocomico River. Postmarked 1907; $15

KINSALE, VA. LOOKING EAST FROM WHARF     PUBL. BY BAILEY & JEFFERIES.
243

The Maryland, Delaware and Virginia Railway Company's steamer *Middlesex*. The handwritten message on the backside reads: "Middlesex leaving Irvington Wharf, Virginia." Circa 1907-12; $25

The steamer *Lancaster* was built in 1892 for the Weems Steamboat Company. In 1905 she came under the ownership of the Maryland, Delaware and Virginia Railway Company. The *Lancaster* is shown here at Wellfords, a landing on the Rappahannock River near Warsaw, Virginia. Postmarked 1914; $30

The steamer *Piankatank* operated between Baltimore, Maryland and Virginia's Piankatank River between the years 1911 and 1932. Circa 1907-12; $15

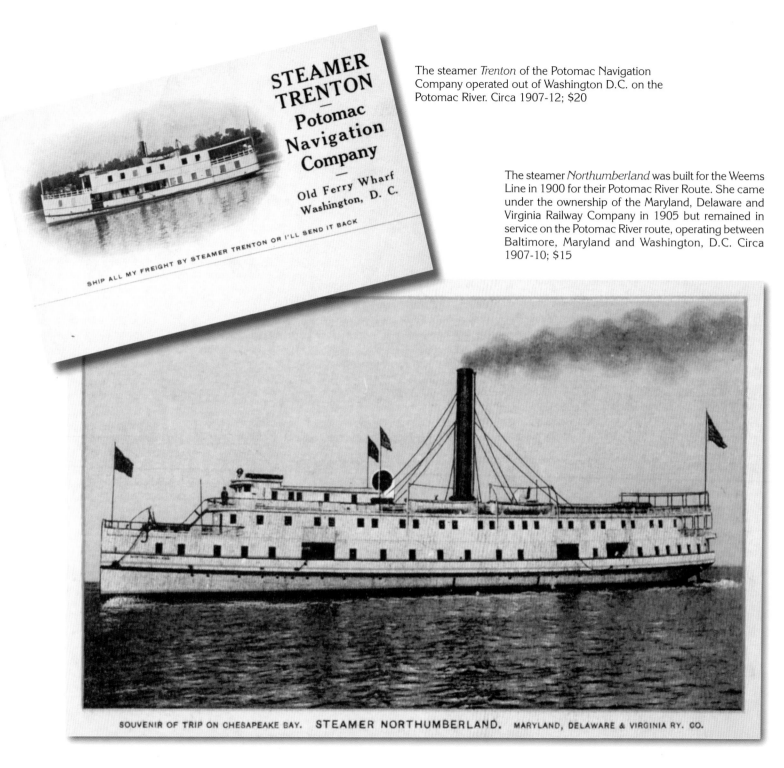

STEAMER TRENTON

Potomac Navigation Company

Old Ferry Wharf Washington, D. C.

SHIP ALL MY FREIGHT BY STEAMER TRENTON OR I'LL SEND IT BACK

The steamer *Trenton* of the Potomac Navigation Company operated out of Washington D.C. on the Potomac River. Circa 1907-12; $20

The steamer *Northumberland* was built for the Weems Line in 1900 for their Potomac River Route. She came under the ownership of the Maryland, Delaware and Virginia Railway Company in 1905 but remained in service on the Potomac River route, operating between Baltimore, Maryland and Washington, D.C. Circa 1907-10; $15

SOUVENIR OF TRIP ON CHESAPEAKE BAY. STEAMER NORTHUMBERLAND. MARYLAND, DELAWARE & VIRGINIA RY. CO.

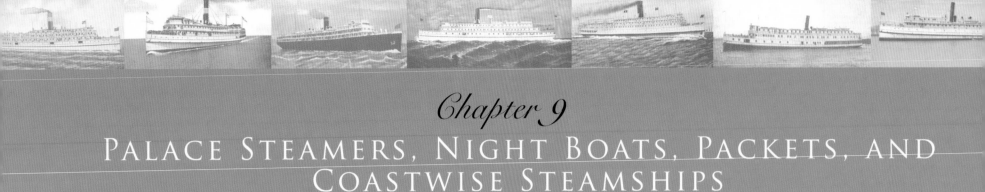

# Chapter 9
## PALACE STEAMERS, NIGHT BOATS, PACKETS, AND COASTWISE STEAMSHIPS

## CHESAPEAKE STEAMSHIP COMPANY

Two celebratory, banner years for the Chesapeake Steamship Company were 1911 and 1913. In 1911, they took possession of two new, sister ships, the *City of Baltimore* and the *City of Norfolk*. The 310-foot, steel hulled vessels were built for the company's Baltimore to Norfolk route by Maryland Steel Company. Two years later, the company took possession of a pair of new, 277-foot, steel hulled sister ships, the *City of Annapolis* and the *City of Richmond*. These latter vessels were placed in service on the company's York River Route which operated between Baltimore and West Point at the head of the York River, with final rail connection to Richmond. The company described its new steamships as: "Floating hotels of the most modern type."

Fog and fire have always been real and present dangers to the mariner. In an era before sophisticated electronics, navigation often depended on the sight, and sometimes quick decision, of a ship's captain. Tragedy by fog was to strike the Chesapeake Steamship Company on February 24, 1927, off the mouth of the Potomac River. Making her way northbound

through a heavy fog, the *City of Annapolis* was struck on her port side by her sister ship, *City of Richmond*, which was on its way down the Bay. There was one fatality aboard the *City of Annapolis*. The *City of Annapolis* began to take on water; her passengers and crew were transferred to the *City of Richmond*. The *City of Annapolis* soon sunk and was a complete loss. Ten years later, on July 29, 1937, tragedy by fire was to strike the steamship line. The *City of Baltimore,* south-bound, caught fire off Seven Point Knoll. The firefighting equipment failed to work correctly. The launch of life rafts was haphazard. In the face of a rapidly intensifying inferno, many passengers had no other choice but to jump overboard. Gallant and heroic attempts were made to rescue passengers and to save the ship, but in the end the ship was a complete loss, burning to the waterline. Three passengers lost their lives.

The Chesapeake Steamship Company originally emerged on the scene in 1900, the result of a reworking of the assets of the defunct Baltimore Chesapeake and Richmond Steamboat Company. From the beginning, the "New Bay

Line," as the company was early referred to, was in direct competition for freight and passengers with the Baltimore Steam Packet Company (Old Bay Line). The competition finally ended in 1941 when the Chesapeake Steamship Company merged with the stronger Old Bay Line. The house flag of the Old Bay Line was soon seen flying from the steamboats that had belonged to its former rival.

The steamships *City of Baltimore* and *City of Norfolk* were built for the Chesapeake Steamship company in 1911. Circa 1915-20; $6

"BALTIMORE" and "CITY of NORFOLK" SISTER SHIPS

Finest Passenger Steamers
on the
Chesapeake Bay

CHESAPEAKE STEAMSHIP COMPANY—BALTIMORE, MD.

The Chesapeake Steamship Company's 298 foot, *City of Norfolk* is shown here underway. Circa 1915-20; $8

The 262 foot *City of Richmond* was built in 1913 for the Chesapeake Steamship Company. Circa 1915-20; $8

The *City of Annapolis* was built for the Chesapeake Steamship Company in 1913. During a fog in 1927 she was involved in a collision with her sister ship, the *City of Richmond* and was sunk. Circa 1915-20; $15

The steamer *Columbia* was built in 1907 for the Chesapeake Steamship Company. Circa 1907; $15

# Merchants and Miners Transportation Company

The Merchants and Miners Transportation Company was established at Baltimore in 1852, with coastwise service between Baltimore and Boston, Massachusetts beginning in 1854. The company name is derived from the fact that its founders envisioned a thriving business transporting general merchandise and mining products. Service to Providence, Rhode Island was added in 1859. In 1876, the Baltimore to Savannah, Georgia line was begun. In addition to freight, passenger traffic was an important part of the company's business. Service was eventually extended to Jacksonville, Miami, and Palm Beach, Florida. In the 1930s, the company was promoting its five new steamships as being especially accommodating to the coastwise tourist trade.

"These sturdy ships, each a city block long, have three decks for passengers, and a number of large public rooms, luxuriously furnished, including a social hall, music room, smoking lounge, and reception hall. The staterooms have hot and cold water, telephone and windows instead of the customary portholes. Many of the rooms have private baths, with salt and fresh water. A newsstand, barber shop and a library of new fiction are among the conveniences. For health, rest and recreation, travel by water."

The five vessels were well received by the public and carried thousands of passengers throughout the 1930s. The vessels were often

On shipboard, the Merchant and Miners Transportation Company. Circa 1926-30; $7

referred to as the "Five Sisters." They were named the *Alleghany, Berkshire, Chatham, Dorchester,* and *Fairfax.*

With the start of the Second World War, coastwise shipping came to a halt. The "Five Sisters" were requisitioned by the War Shipping Administration. None of the vessels were ever to do service for the company again. By the war's end, the vessels had been sunk, worn out, or scattered to distant ports. The *Chatham* was the first casualty, going to the bottom of the ocean in 1942. The *Fairfax,* war scarred, ended up being sold to the Chinese.

The *Dorchester* is best remembered as the ship of the "Four Chaplains." In 1943, off Greenland, the *Dorchester* was the victim of a German torpedo. The four chaplains of three faiths gave up their lifebelts so that they could be used by others. The chaplains were last seen standing shoulder to shoulder on the ship's rail as she sank beneath the waves.

The company never recovered from the loss of business during the Second World War and the loss of its "Five Sisters." Building new ships was beyond the company's means. At war's end, East Coast shipping was being dominated by truck and rail lines. The company languished for several more years, but mostly in name and memory only. Finally, the decision to dissolve the company was made in May of 1948.

During the years of the company, the Merchant and Miners Transportation Company had two ships with the name *Dorchester*. The first was built in 1889, the second in 1926. Here we see the Officers of the first *Dorchester*. Circa 1907-12; $15

Upper deck of the steamship *Dorchester* of the Merchant and Miners Transportation Company. Circa 1907-12; $15

S. S. "DORCHESTER" MERCHANTS AND MINERS TRANSPORTATION CO.

The dining room of the Merchant and Miners Transportation Company's steamship *Howard*. The *Howard* was built in 1895. Postmarked 1907; $15

The steamship *Dorchester* was built in 1926 for the Merchant and Miners Transportation Company. She was the company's second *Dorchester*, the first having been built in 1889. In 1943, while in service as a troop transport in the North Atlantic the *Dorchester* was struck by an enemy torpedo. Over 600 men lost their lives, including the heroic four chaplains that refused to get into the lifeboats so that others could do so. Circa 1930s; $8

# Norfolk and Washington Steamboat Company

With the objective of offering reliable, first-class service between the two cities that make up their company name, the Norfolk and Washington Steamship Company was incorporated in 1890. Two ships, the *Washington* and the *Norfolk*, built to the same specifications by Harland and Hollingsworth of Wilmington, Delaware, were delivered to the company in 1891. The company advertised that its posh and polished vessels "Create a New Era in Potomac River and Chesapeake Bay Navigation" and referred to them as "Palace Steamers." The route down the Potomac River, the western shore of the Chesapeake Bay from Smith Point to Fort Monroe and into Hampton Roads, was a distance of 196 miles. A 1910 company timetable has the southbound steamer leaving Washington at 6:45 P.M. and arriving at Norfolk at 8:00 A.M. The northbound steamer left Norfolk at 6:00 P.M. with a 7:00 A.M. arrival at Washington. During a heavy fog, the company's *District of Columbia* was involved in an accident with a tanker in October 1948. Repairs to the vessel being too costly, the company elected to cease operations in December 1948. The *District of Columbia* was later sold to the Baltimore Steam Packet Company. After the ship had been repaired and refurbished, the ship's new owners returned her to service on her old route between Norfolk and Washington.

The 291 foot steamer *Southland* was built for the Norfolk and Washington Steamboat Company in 1908. Circa 1908; $45

The 246 foot steamer *Washington* was built for the Norfolk and Washington steamboat Company in 1891. In 1910 she was sold to Colonial Navigation Company and renamed *Lexington*. Circa 1907; $10

The 291 foot steamer *Northland* was built in 1911 for the Norfolk and Washington Steamboat Company. In 1942 she was requisitioned by the War Shipping Administration and left the Chesapeake's waters forever.

Steamer *Southland* of the Norfolk and Washington Steamboat Company. Circa 1930s; $15

The 291 foot *District of Columbia* was launched in 1924 for the Norfolk and Washington Steamboat Company. In 1948 she collided with the tanker *Georgia* in Hampton Roads. In 1949 she was purchased by the Baltimore Steam Packet Company, rebuilt and put back into service on the Norfolk – Washington, D.C. route. Circa 1930s; $15

# The Baltimore Steam Packet Company (Old Bay Line)

The Baltimore Steam Packet Company celebrated its centennial year in 1940. It had the distinction of being the oldest steamboat company operating in the United States. The Old Bay Line, as the company was popularly known, was nothing less than a Chesapeake Bay tradition with its daily, overnight sailings between Baltimore, Old Point Comfort, and Norfolk. Northbound and southbound steamers each left their respective docks at 6:30 P.M. with arrivals early the next morning at opposite ends of the Bay. The steamers were known as "Night Boats." The average twelve-hour trip afforded one just enough time to settle in and relax, have a late evening meal, and a full night of rest in a private stateroom. A June, 1938 company timetable states that the one way fare was $4.00 with a round trip ticket, good for thirty days, costing $6.00. A "De Luxe Table d'Hote Dinner" could be had for $1.25. If one desired to take their automobile ("Saves a 230 mile drive"), it was an extra $4.00. In its centennial year the company was operating with three well-appointed vessels, the *State of Maryland*, *State of Virginia*, and the *President Warfield*. Plans were in the works for the company to absorb the assets of its long time rival, the Chesapeake Steamship Company. When that happened in 1941, the company had six vessels at its disposal. This luxury was short lived; in 1942 the War Shipping Administration requisitioned the *State of Maryland*, *State of Virginia*, *President Warfield*, and the *Yorktown*. This left the company with the older, less desirable *City of Norfolk* and *City of Richmond*. The company was able to purchase the *District of Columbia* from the Norfolk & Washington Steamboat company when that company ceased operations in 1949. The *District of Columbia* was placed back on her old route between Norfolk and Washington and was also used as a relief boat for the Baltimore to Norfolk run. Service to Washington had to be curtailed in 1957 because the government pier there was in such disrepair. The government closed its dock at Old Point Comfort in 1959. High labor cost, the loss of its Washington route, the closure of the Old Point Comfort dock, competition for freight with trucking companies, and upkeep of aging vessels were serious problems for the company. The company decided to cease operations in 1962. Travel by night boat on the Chesapeake came to an end in April of that year with the *City of Norfolk* making the last run from Norfolk to Baltimore.

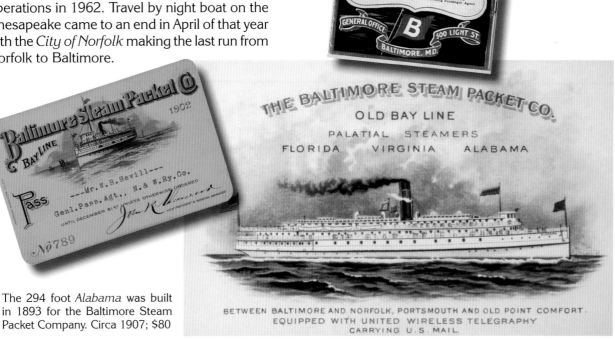

The 294 foot *Alabama* was built in 1893 for the Baltimore Steam Packet Company. Circa 1907; $80

The Baltimore Steam Packet Co.
(Old Bay Line)

Between Baltimore, Old Point Comfort "Fortress Monroe," Norfolk and
Portsmouth, Va. Daily Except Sunday.

Magnificent Steamers "Virginia" "New" "Alabama" and "Georgia"

Superb Equipment and "Menu"

Comfort, Safety, Speed, Pleasure.

Direct Route to Jamestown Exposition, Opens April 26th, Closes October 30th, 1907.

The 296 foot *Virginia* was built in 1905 for the Baltimore Steam Packet Company. Circa 1907; $60

Interior views of the Baltimore Steam Packet Company's steamers *Alabama* and *Florida*. The handwritten message on the backside reads: "10-21-21, 6:30 P.M. aboard ship, on my way home honey. This time to Baltimore. Saturday won't come too soon. Love, Billy." Circa 1922; $20

122

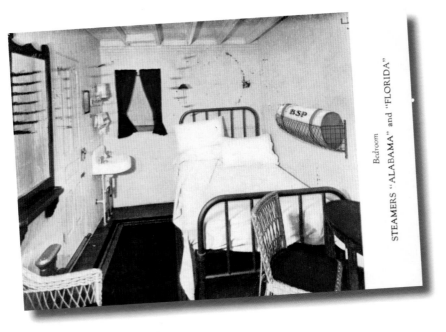

Bedroom – Baltimore Steam Packet Company's steamers *Alabama* and *Florida*. The handwritten message on the backside reads: "Norfolk, VA, 5-8-22 Arrived safely, best wishes to all, Henry." Circa 1922; $20

Main Saloon and Gallery – Baltimore Steam Packet Company's steamers *Alabama* and *Florida*. The handwritten message on the backside reads: "On my way to Old Point." Postmarked 1922; $20

New steamers, *State of Maryland* and *State of Virginia*. The Baltimore Steam Packet Company had the 320 foot *State of Maryland* built in 1922 and the 320 foot *State of Virginia* built in 1923. Both vessels were requisitioned by the War Shipping Administration in 1942. By the end of the war the vessels were too worn out to be of any use to the company. Circa 1923; $15

Interior views of the Baltimore Steam Packet Company's *State of Maryland* and *State of Virginia*. Circa 1923; $15

FORWARD SALOON AND GALLERIES

Dining room – new steamer *State of Virginia*, Baltimore Steam Packet Company. Circa 1923; $10

The forward saloon and galleries, Baltimore Steam Packet Company's *State of Maryland* and *State of Virginia*. The handwritten message on the backside reads: "Started back from Norfolk, VA, Sept. 25 at 6:30 P.M. Arrived in Baltimore 7:00 A.M. Sept. 26, 14 hrs. on water." Circa 1923; $15

Dancing on board new steamers *State of Maryland* and *State of Virginia*, Baltimore Steam Packet Company. Circa 1923; $10

DANCING ON BOARD NEW STEAMERS—BALTIMORE STEAM PACKET CO. (OLD BAY LINE)

STEAMER PRESIDENT WARFIELD.

The 320 foot *President Warfield* was built in 1928 for the Baltimore Steam Packet Company. She was requisitioned by the War Shipping Administration in 1942. After WWII she was returned to U.S. waters and was about ready to be scrapped when she was purchased by a clandestine Jewish organization in Palestine with intentions of bringing thousands of Jewish refugees from France to Palestine. *President Warfield* was renamed *Exodus 1947* and sailed for France. From France, with over 4,500 Jewish refugees on board, the ship sailed for Palestine. British destroyers intercepted the ship. The refugees were removed and returned to France. The ship became a symbol of the Jewish struggle for an independent state. Postmarked 1932; $15

# The Baltimore & Philadelphia Steamboat Company
## (The Ericsson Line)

The Baltimore & Philadelphia Steamboat Company, also known as the Ericsson Line, was incorporated in 1844. Its vessels operated between Baltimore and Philadelphia by way of the Chesapeake & Delaware Canal. A familiar phrase seen in the company's advertising was "By River, Lock and Bay." A company brochure from 1907 informed the traveler that night steamers left daily, except Sunday, from Philadelphia and Baltimore at 5:00 P.M. The night boat from Baltimore would arrive at Philadelphia at 7:00 the next morning. The arrival time at Baltimore for the night boat from Philadelphia was 6 A.M. Traversing the canal and navigating through its three locks took approximately three and a half hours of the voyage. The steamers *Anthony Groves, Jr.*, built in 1893, and the *Ericsson*, built in 1897, made the overnight trips. Stops were made along the way at Chester, Delaware City, St. Georges, Chesapeake City, Town Point, and Betterton. Cabin fare was $2.00 and deck (second class) was $1.50. Meals were served "table de hote" at 50 cents each. The company also operated day steamers between Baltimore and Philadelphia. The daylight runs were made with the company's newer steamers, *Penn* and *Lord Baltimore*.

Due to the narrowness of the canal and its locks, the steamers of the Ericsson Line had all been screw-propelled and were built with narrow beams. After the widening of the canal was completed in 1927, it was no longer necessary to have a narrow beam. The last steamer built for the company in 1926 was the *John Cadwalader*. The vessel was 219 feet in length and had a beam of 43 feet. Interesting when compared to the steamers *Penn* and *Lord Baltimore* which were sister ships, built in 1903, each with a length of 196 feet and a beam of 23.5 feet.

The *Lord Baltimore* was built for the Baltimore and Philadelphia Steamboat Company in 1902. Circa 1907; $40

The 209 foot *Anthony Groves Jr.* was built in 1893 for the Baltimore and Philadelphia Steamboat Company. Postmarked 1907; $20

Steamer Anthony Groves, Jr.

The 219 foot *John Cadwalader* was built in 1926 for the Baltimore and Philadelphia Steamboat Company. She operated between Baltimore and Philadelphia by way of the Chesapeake and Delaware Canal. Circa 1926; $10

The steamer *John Cadwalader* passes under the lift bridge at St. Georges, Delaware on her way between Baltimore and Philadelphia by way of the Chesapeake and Delaware Canal. Circa 1926; $10

A group aboard the steamer *John Cadwalader* of the Baltimore and Philadelphia Steamboat Company. Circa 1926; $10

The dining room of the steamer *John Cadwalader* of the Baltimore and Philadelphia Steamboat Company. Circa 1926; $10

The gallery deck aboard the steamer *John Cadwalader* of the
Baltimore and Philadelphia Steamboat Company. Circa 1926; $10

The salon deck aboard the steamer *John Cadwalader*
of the Baltimore and Philadelphia Steamboat Company. Circa 1926; $10

The palm room aboard the steamer *John Cadwalader*
of the Baltimore and Philadelphia Steamboat Company.
Circa 1926; $10

# The Old Dominion Steamship Company (Old Dominion Line)

The Old Dominion Steamship Company, otherwise known as the Old Dominion Line, was organized in 1867. The company offered daily service to and from Norfolk and New York City. The year 1907 was an especially busy one for the company, as it was the year that the well attended Jamestown Exposition was held at the Seawell's Point area of Norfolk. The company had five sleek, ocean going vessels: the *Jamestown*, *Jefferson*, *Hamilton*, *Princess Anne*, and *Monroe*. They were being used alternately to make the daily, 19 hour, 328 mile coastwise run between the two ports. At the time, 1907, a round trip ticket cost $10.00 and that included a stateroom berth (sleeping accommodations). Departure from Norfolk was at 8 P.M. with a New York arrival time at 3:30 P.M. on the following day. Departure from New York was at 3 P.M. with arrival at Norfolk in the mid morning of the following day.

The 4,700 ton, screw propelled *Monroe* was built in 1903 for the Old Dominion Steamship Company. She sailed between Norfolk and New York, alternating her days with other vessels of the company. Circa 1903-07; $8

The 4,000 ton, screw propelled *Hamilton* was built in 1899 for the Old Dominion Steamship Company. She sailed between Norfolk and New York, alternating her days with other vessels of the company. Circa 1903-07; $8

129

The 4,000 ton, screw propelled *Jefferson* was built in 1899 for the Old Dominion Steamship Company. She sailed between Norfolk and New York, alternating her days with other vessels of the company. Circa 1903-07; $8

The 3,000 ton, screw propelled *Jamestown* was built in 1894 for the Old Dominion Steamship Company. She sailed between Norfolk and New York, alternating her days with other vessels of the company. Circa 1903-07; $8

The steamer *Brandon* and her sister ship *Berkeley* operated on the James River for the Old Dominion Steamship Company. The ships alternated on the route between Norfolk and Richmond, Virginia. Departure from Norfolk was at 7 P.M. with arrival at Richmond, Virginia at 6 A.M. From Richmond the steamer would leave at 7 P.M. and arrive at Norfolk, Virginia at 6 A.M. Circa 1910; $8

OLD DOMINION LINE.
DAILY SERVICE BETWEEN NEW YORK AND VIRGINIA.

The steamer *Berkley* and her sister ship *Brandon* operated on the James River for the Old Dominion Steamship Company. The ships alternated on the route between Norfolk and Richmond, Virginia. Departure from Norfolk was at 7 P.M. with arrival at Richmond, Virginia at 6 A.M. From Richmond the steamer would leave at 7 P.M. and arrive at Norfolk, Virginia at 6 A.M. Circa 1910; $8

For the men that harvest the bounty of the Chesapeake Bay's seafood for a living, the work is hard and the hours are long. The monetary rewards at times are disappointing and at best unpredictable. The weather can be unmerciful. Sudden summer storms are a danger. Ice and cold in the winter make work hazardous and hard. Why do they do it? They are an independent breed. They do it because working the water is in their blood. Their fathers worked the water. Their father's fathers worked the water. It's the life they were brought up to do. It's the way of life that they will pass on to their children.

Unloading a crab boat at Crisfield, Maryland. Postmarked 1909; $20

Crab Boats, Crisfield, Md.

132

A man in a crab skiff near Davis Wharf, Virginia. Circa 1909; $12

Transferring oysters from boat to packing house at Crisfield, Maryland. Postmarked 1917; $12

Hand tonging for oysters on the Chester River, near Chestertown, Maryland. Circa 1930s; $10

Workboats at Crisfield, Maryland. Circa 1909; $12

Oyster shucking is done by hand, one oyster at a time. Circa 1904-07; $8

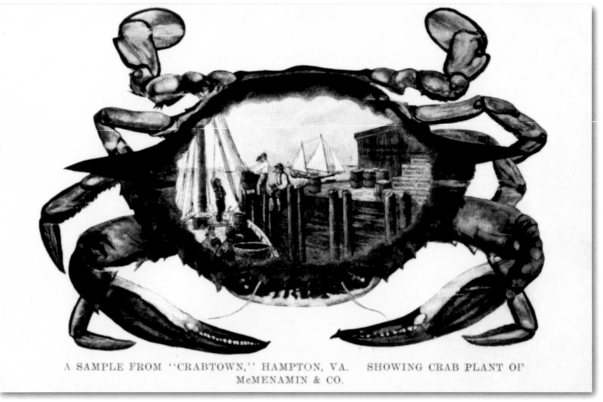

A SAMPLE FROM "CRABTOWN," HAMPTON, VA.  SHOWING CRAB PLANT OF McMENAMIN & CO.

The process of canning crab meat was perfected at Hampton, Virginia in the 1870s. Circa 1904-07; $15

Hand tonging for oysters. Circa 1904-07; $8

A James River Oyster Boat, near Hampton, Va.

Returning with a full load of oysters, near Hampton, Virginia. Circa 1909-12; $8

POUND FISHERMEN, MATHEWS, VA.

Pound fishermen, pursing the seine, near Mathews, Virginia. Circa 1930s; $8

Piles of oyster shells from the packing houses at Hampton, Virginia. Circa 1907-12; $15

Oyster canning factory at Crisfield, Maryland. Postmarked 1916; $15

Wm. B. McCaddin & Co., Fish and Oysters, Irma Brand, Baltimore, Maryland. Circa 1907-12; $20

Tilghman Packing Company, oyster and crab packers, Tilghman, Maryland. Circa 1907; $30

Oyster wharf at Pratt Street, Baltimore, Maryland. Circa 1904-07; $12

Soft shell crab packing room at Crisfield, Maryland. Postmarked 1910; $20

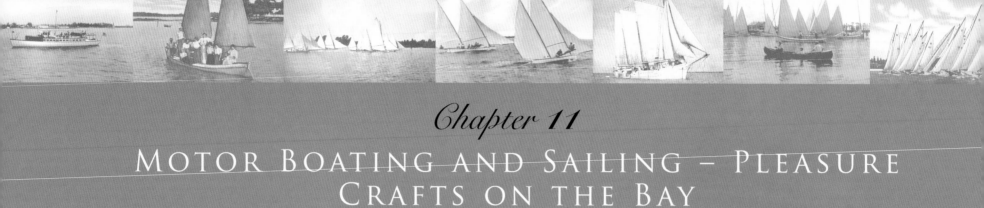

So what do you do if you have a boat and want to be around others who have boats? The answer, for many, is to join the local yacht club. As a member, you make friends, exchange boating information, sharpen your nautical skills and take part in the yearly regatta where you race your boat against other similar boats.

Yacht clubs have a long tradition on the Chesapeake. A sampling of the rivers in the Bay region that have lent their names to be a part of a yacht club's official title are: the North East, Miles, Tred Avon, Elk, Chester, Bush, Rappahannock, and Sassafras. The earliest yacht club in Maryland, the Maryland Club, was formed in 1857. The Old Dominion Boat Club was formed, as the name implies, in Virginia in 1880. The Annapolis Yacht Club dates back to 1886. The Maryland Yacht Club was founded in 1908.

So what do you do if you have a boat but not the desire to join the local yacht club? The answer of course is obvious, simply enjoy the time you spend on your boat cruising the Chesapeake's waters.

A motor yacht in the harbor at St. Michaels, Maryland. Postmarked 1909; $10

A motor yacht on the Tred Avon river at Oxford, Maryland. Circa 1930s; $8

The sailboat *Nighthawk* under full sail in the harbor at Urbanna, Virginia. Circa 1930s; $8

A group enjoys themselves on the West River, near West River, Maryland. Postmarked 1909; $8

Log canoe sailboats racing on the Miles River at St. Michaels, Maryland. Circa 1907; $15

Star boats racing off of Gibson Island, Maryland. Postmarked 1956; $6

Chesapeake Bay log canoes racing on the Miles River off of St. Michaels, Maryland. Circa 1930s; $6

The boat race is either over or getting ready to start at Colonial Beach, Virginia. Postmarked 1909; $10

A sailing vacation on the Chesapeake Bay had its appeal. Circa 1940; $7

The 128 foot schooner *Levin J. Marvel* offered week long sailing vacations on the Chesapeake Bay. The handwritten message on the backside reads: "Cabins are on the port side. We are now sailing up the Choptank River to Cambridge. Just finished dinner, all well, weather good, 10 passengers." Postmarked 1950; $8

Crossing the Line. Yacht Races near Oxford, Maryland. Circa 1908-15; $7

Sailboating on the Chesapeake near Havre de Grace, Maryland. Circa 1940s; $7

The Ariel Rowing Club, Ferry Bar, Baltimore, Maryland. Circa 1909; $8

The Yacht Club at Chesapeake City, Maryland. Postmarked 1941; $15

The Arundel Boat Club near Baltimore,
Maryland. Circa 1908-12; $8

The Baltimore Yacht Club, Baltimore,
Maryland. Circa 1916-1925. $8

Watching the Boat Races at Cambridge,
Maryland. Postmarked 1915; $10

The Regatta at St. Michaels, Maryland.
Circa 1904-07; $10

Yachting on Chesapeake Bay near Baltimore, Md.

Yachting on the Chesapeake Bay, near Baltimore, Maryland. Postmarked 1942; $4

Hampton Roads Yacht Club, Willoughby Beach, near Norfolk, Va.

Hampton Roads Yacht Club at Willoughby Beach, near Norfolk, Virginia. Circa 1910; $8

Newspaper Launch, Colonial Beach, Va.

A small motor boat, typical for the time period, at Colonial Beach, Virginia. Circa 1915; $15

BOATING AT BETTERTON, MD.

Boating at Betterton, Maryland. Circa 1910; $10

## Chapter 12
# SHIP BUILDING AND SHIPYARDS

Wooden shipbuilding was once an important industry on the Chesapeake. Traditional vessels like the skipjack, bugeye, brogan, and pungy were built by craftsmen at many small shipyards in the Bay area. Baltimore was home to a number of shipyards that built larger vessels. One of these, the shipyard of the Maryland Steel Company, built a number of vessels for the local steamboat companies. In 1917, the Maryland Steel Company was bought by Bethlehem Steel Corporation and became their Sparrows Point, Maryland shipyard. Up the Patapsco River at Fairfield and at the site of the former Baltimore Dry Dock & Shipbuilding Co., Bethlehem-Fairfield Shipyards, Inc. was established in 1940. The shipyard was vital during the Second World War, and employed upwards of 27,000 people during that period. Between the years 1941 and 1945, 508 Liberty ships were built. This was a monumental number, considering that each Liberty Ship was over 440 feet in length.

The Newport News Shipbuilding & Dry Dock Company located at Newport News, Virginia is the largest private shipyard in the United States. The company has been in continuous operation since 1891. The Norfolk & Washington Steamboat Company had the 247-foot *Newport News* built by the shipyard in 1895. In 1906 the shipyard built the *Jamestown*, a 262-foot pas-senger steamer for the company. The shipyard built the three passenger ships, the *Chatham*, *Dorchester*, and *Fairfax* for the Merchant & Miners Transportation Company in 1925 and 1926. The ill-fated, 508-foot, luxury ocean liner *Morro Castle* was built at the shipyard in 1930. During the Second World War upwards of 35,000 people were employed at the shipyard. Among the shipyard's accomplishments during the Second World War was the building of seven aircraft carriers.

A crowd turns out to watch a large wooden ship being launched at Pocomoke City, Maryland. Circa 1909-12; $15

A proud day at Crisfield, Maryland was the launching of the *Helen Avetta*. Postmarked 1909; $15

A large wooden ship being built at the Deibert Boat Yard in Elkton, Maryland. Postmarked 1906; $15

The launching of a large vessel at Pocomoke City, Maryland. Postmarked 1907; $15

Repairing oyster boats at Crisfield, Maryland. Circa 1907-12; $15

A battleship being prepared for launching at the Newport News Shipbuilding and Dry Dock Company, Newport News, Virginia. Circa 1907-09; $10

Employees swarm the backside of the main office building at the Newport News Shipping and Dry Dock Company to collect their weekly pay. Circa 1905; $8

A large ship sits high and dry in the dry dock at the Newport News Shipbuilding and Dry Dock Company, Newport News, Virginia. Circa 1907; $8

Two military ships are shown in the big dry dock at the Newport News Shipbuilding and Dry Dock Company, Newport News, Virginia. Circa 1907-09; $15

Preparing to launch the battleship *U.S.S. Pennsylvania* on March 16, 1915, at the Newport News Shipbuilding and Dry Dock Company, Newport News, Virginia. The *U.S.S. Pennsylvania* was commissioned 3 months later and was the 10th battleship to be built by the shipbuilder. Circa 1915; $20

The *S.S. Missouri*, a cargo ship, is shown being launched in 1903 at Maryland Steel Company's, Sparrows Point shipyard. The shipyard came under the control of the Bethlehem Steel Corporation in 1917. Circa 1907; $10

Battleship in dry dock at the Norfolk Navy Yard, Norfolk, Virginia. Circa 1916-20. $7

The Old Dominion Line steamship *Berkeley* in dry dock and two other steamships at the Smith & McCoy shipyard at Norfolk, Virginia. Circa 1912-16; $10

*Chapter 13*
# MILITARY MEN AND FORTS

The United States Naval Academy is located at Annapolis, Maryland. Every summer the Naval Academy welcomes a batch of new recruits with ambitions of becoming naval officers. Some of the training these first-year students, "plebes," receive takes place on the Severn River aboard small sailboats and power boats, in which basic lessons in seamanship, navigation, and boat handling are learned.

Fort Monroe is located on a beautiful point of land at the mouth of Hampton Roads and on the Chesapeake Bay known as Old Point Comfort, Virginia. The site was first garrisoned in 1823, and the fort was completed in 1834. Originally called Fortress Monroe, the fort is named for President James Monroe. From 1831 to 1834, Robert E. Lee was stationed at the fort, as was Edgar Allan Poe in 1828. During the Civil War, as many as 6,000 troops were stationed at the fort. Fort Monroe is still an active Army post.

Midshipmen learning seamanship at the United States Naval Academy in Annapolis, Maryland. The *U.S.S. Santee* was used as a training ship until 1912 and is shown in the background. Circa 1907-12; $8

The *Bagley* (*Torpedo Boat No. 24*), built in 1900, came to Annapolis, Maryland in 1907 to spend 8 months as a training ship at the United States Naval Academy. Circa 1907; $10

United States Naval Academy midshipmen practicing their seamanship and rowing skills aboard cutter boats. Circa 1907-12; $8

Midshipmen practice aboard a cutter boat at the United States Naval Academy in Annapolis, Maryland. Circa 1909-12; $10

Midshipmen at the United States Naval Academy waiting to board the ship that will be their home for the summer. Circa 1907-12; $10

Reina Mercedes, Spanish Warship, now used as a
Training Ship, U. S. Naval Academy. Annapolis, Md.

Charles G. Feldmeyer.

OLD FORT SEVERN. NAVAL ACADEMY.

Annapolis, Md.

The 278 foot *Reina Mercedes,* built in 1887 was used as a station
ship at the United States Naval Academy from 1912 until being decommissioned in 1957. Circa 1912; $8

In 1808 Fort Severn was built overlooking the Severn River at
Annapolis, Maryland. The Fort and its 10 acres came under the
control of the Navy in 1845 and a part of the United States Naval
Academy in 1850. Circa 1904-07; $10

U. S.
Receiving Ship "Franklin,"
and Fleet of Steam Launches,
Norfolk, Va.

BAND CONCERT

HOTEL CHAMBERLIN
GEO. F. ADAMS, MGR.
EAST FRONT
FORTRESS MONROE, VA.

The receiving ship, *U.S.S. Franklin* and a fleet of steam
launches, Norfolk, Virginia. Circa 1912-16; $8

The Hotel Chamberlin at Fort Monroe and Old Point
Comfort, Virginia. Circa 1907-12; $8

Viewing the Naval fleet from the sun parlor of the Hotel Chamberlin at Fort Monroe, Virginia. Circa 1907-12; $8

Hotel Chamberlin at Old Point Comfort, Virginia. Circa 1907-12; $8

The 456 foot battleship *U.S.S. Connecticut* in Hampton Roads, near Old Point Comfort, Virginia. Circa 1914; $10

The Norfolk Navy Yard at Portsmouth, Virginia. Circa 1916-25; $7

U. S. NAVAL OPERATING BASE. HAMPTON ROADS. VA.
Boat Drill.

TARGET PRACTICE WITH 13-INCH GUN AT FORTRESS MONROE, VA.

Boat drill at the U.S. Naval Operations
Base, Hampton, Virginia. Circa 1930s; $7

Target practice with the mammoth
defense guns was conducted several times a year at Fort Monroe,
Virginia. Circa 1915-20; $10

Air view of Fort McHenry on the Patapsco
River at Baltimore, Maryland. The birthplace of the Star Spangled Banner. Circa
1940s; $7

AIRVIEW OF FORT McHENRY, BIRTHPLACE
OF STAR SPANGLED BANNER, BALTIMORE, MD.

Looking south on Light Street in Baltimore,
Maryland. Circa 1904; $10

Pay day for the stevedores at Baltimore, Maryland. Circa 1904-07; $10

The busy harbor at Baltimore, Maryland. Circa 1907-12; $8

A large wooden sailing vessel at Baltimore, Maryland. Circa 1902-05; $8

The city dock looking towards Spa Creek at Annapolis, Maryland. Circa 1909; $12

At the foot of the city dock at Annapolis, Maryland. Circa 1909-12; $15

Birdseye view of Georgetown, Md.

The Sassafras River waterfront at Georgetown, Maryland. Circa 1907-12; $12

Wicomico Harbor, Salisbury, Md.

Samuel P. Woodcock, reliable Real Estate Dealer in attractive farm lands, Salisbury, Md.

Wooden sailing craft in the harbor at Salisbury, Maryland. Circa 1904-07; $12

WATERFRONT ST. MICHAELS, MARYLAND

Workboats along the waterfront at St. Michaels, Maryland. Circa 1930s; $10

View of Harbor, Solomons, Md.

Along the waterfront at Solomons, Maryland. Circa 1920s; $15

Urbanna, Virginia, from the Sky, Looking North

A view of the Rappahannock River at Urbanna, Virginia. Postmarked 1924; $12

No. 5—"Commodore Maury" leaving Irvington Wharf.

The wharf at Irvington, Virginia. Circa 1907-12; $15

A busy time at the steamboat wharf at Irvington, Virginia. Circa 1907-12; $15

The Baltimore Steam Packet Company's pier at Norfolk, Virginia. Circa 1907-09; $15

The harbor at Tangier Island, Virginia. Circa 1950s; $15

The Chesapeake and Ohio Railway Piers at Newport News, Virginia. Circa 1907-12; $15

The harbor draped in moonlight at Cape Charles, Virginia. Circa 1915-25; $10

A large vessel passes the Baltimore & Ohio Railroad piers at Locust Point, Baltimore, Maryland. Postmarked 1909; $10

OLD BOAT HOUSE, JONES' CREEK
As seen en route to Bay Shore Park

Easton Point by moonlight, Easton, Maryland. Postmarked 1909; $15

An old Boat House on Jones' Creek. A view from the trolley car as it meandered its way from downtown Baltimore out to the amusement park and bathing beach at Bay Shore Park, Maryland. Postmarked 1908; $7

EASTON POINT BY MOONLIGHT, EASTON, Md.

157

Along the Susquehanna River, Havre de Grace, Maryland. Circa 1907-12; $15

Boat Houses, Havre de Grace, Maryland. Circa 1907-12; $15

Waterfront, Hampton Institute, Virginia. Circa 1930s; $6

On the beach, Newport News, Virginia. Circa 1904-07; $8

Brome's Wharf on St. Mary's River, St. Mary's City, Maryland. Circa 1907-12; $12

Oyster boats in Cove Landing, Crisfield, Maryland. Circa 1907-12. $20

Children vacationing in Mathews County, Virginia. Circa 1940s; $8

The steamer *Penn* leaving Town Point, Maryland. She was built in 1902 for the Baltimore and Philadelphia Steamboat Company. Here the *Penn* is shown in all her panchromatic glory, frozen by camera and film, forever navigating the upper waters of the Chesapeake Bay. Postmarked 1909; $20

# BIBLIOGRAPHY

Beitzell, Edwin W. *Life on the Potomac River.* Abell, Maryland: E. W. Beitzell, 1968.

Brewington, M. V. *Chesapeake Bay: A Pictorial Maritime History*, Cambridge, Maryland: Cornell Maritime Press, Inc., 1953.

Brewington, M. V. *Chesapeake Bay Log Canoes and Bugeyes.* Cambridge, Maryland: Cornell Maritime Press, Inc., 1963.

Brown, Alexander C. *The Old Bay Line, 1840-1940.* New York: Bonanaza Books, 1940.

Brown, Alexander C. *Steam Packets on the Chesapeake: A History of the Old Bay Line Since 1840.* Cambridge, Maryland: Cornell Maritime Press, Inc., 1965.

Brown, Alexander C. *The Good Ships of Newport News.* Cambridge, Maryland: Tidewater Publishers, 1976.

Burgess, Robert H. *This Was Chesapeake Bay.* Cambridge, Maryland: Cornell Maritime Press, Inc., 1963.

Burgess, Robert H. *Chesapeake Circle.* Cambridge, Maryland: Cornell Maritime Press, 1965.

Burgess, Robert H., and Wood, H. Graham. *Steamboats Out of Baltimore.* Cambridge, Maryland: Tidewater Publishers, 1968.

DeGast, Robert. *The Lighthouses of the Chesapeake.* Baltimore, Maryland: Johns Hopkins University Press, 1973.

Elliott, Richard V. *Last of the Steamboats: The Saga of the Wilson Line.* Cambridge, Maryland: Tidewater Publishers, 1970.

Hain, John A. *Side Wheel Steamers of the Chesapeake Bay, 1880-1947.* Glen Burnie, Maryland: Glendale Press, 1947.

Hilton, George W. *The Night Boat.* Berkeley, California: Howell-North Books, 1968.

Holly, David C. *Steamboat on the Chesapeake, Emma Giles and the Tolchester Line.* Centreville, Maryland: Tidewater Publishers, 1987.

Holly, David C. *Tidewater By Steamboat, A Saga of the Chesapeake.* Baltimore, Maryland: The Johns Hopkins University Press, 1991.

Holly, David C. *Chesapeake Steamboats, Vanished Fleet.* Centreville, Maryland: Tidewater Publishers, 1994.

Hornberger, Patrick, and Turbyville, Linda. *Forgotten Beacons, The Lost Lighthouses of the Chesapeake Bay.* Annapolis, Maryland: Eastwind Publishing, 1997.

Jones, Harry, and Jones, Timothy. *Night Boat on the Potomac, A History of the Norfolk and Washington Steamboat Company.* Providence, Rhode Island: The Steamship Historical Society of America, Inc., 1996.

Keith, Robert C. *Baltimore Harbor: A Picture History.* Baltimore, Maryland: Ocean World Publishing Co., 1982.

Lang, Varley. *Follow the Water.* Winston-Salem, North Carolina: John F. Blair, Publisher, 1961.

*Merchant Vessels of the United States: 1891.* Washington, D.C.: Government Printing Office, 1891.

Ryan, Dorothy B. *Picture Postcards in the United States, 1893-1918.* New York, New York: Clarkson N. Potter, Inc. / Publisher, 1982.

Stensvaag, James T. *Hampton, From the Sea to the Stars.* Virginia Beach, Virginia: The Donning Company / Publishers, 1985.

Tazewell, William L. *Newport News Shipbuilding, The First Century.* Newport News, Virginia: The Mariners' Museum, 1986.

Turbyville, Linda. *Bay Beacons, Lighthouses of the Chesapeake Bay.* Annapolis, Maryland: Eastwind Publishing, 1995.

Wertenbaker, Thomas J. *Norfolk: Historic Southern Port.* Durham, North Carolina: Duke University Press, 1931.

Williams, Ames W. *Otto Mears Goes East, The Chesapeake Beach Railway.* Prince Frederick, Maryland: Calvert County Historical Society, 1975.

Wilson, John C. *Virginia's Northern Neck, A Pictorial History.* Virginia Beach, Virginia: The Donning Company / Publishers, 1984.